My Sovereign, My Sin, My Salvation

Bert Thompson, Ph.D.

APOLOGETICS PRESS

Apologetics Press, Inc.

230 Landmark Drive

Montgomery, Alabama 36117-2752

© Copyright 1999

ISBN: 0-932859-35-6

All rights reserved. No part of this book may be reproduced in any form without permission from the publisher, except in the case of brief quotations embodied in articles or critical reviews.

TABLE OF CONTENTS

1
INTRODUCTION

The academic discipline of Christian apologetics is concerned with offering a reasoned defense of historical, New Testament Christianity. The English word "apology" derives from the Greek *apologia*, which means to "defend" or "make a defense." Various biblical writers acknowledged the legitimacy of such activity. The apostle Peter, for example, wrote:

> But sanctify in your hearts Christ as Lord: being ready always to give answer [Greek, *apologian*] to every man that asketh you a reason concerning the hope that is in you, yet with meekness and fear (1 Peter 3:15).

Paul, in his epistle to the Philippians, stated that he was "set for the defense [Greek, *apologian*] of the Gospel" (Philippians 1:16). Paul's writings, in fact, teem with sound arguments that provide a rational undergirding for his readers' faith. Christianity is not some kind of vague, emotionally based belief system intended for unthinking simpletons. Rather, it is a logical system of thought that can be both defended and accepted by analytical minds.

In any defense of Christianity, a variety of evidence can be employed. Such evidence may be derived from science, philosophy, or history, to list just a few examples. It is not uncommon to hear someone mention studies within the field of "Christian evidences." Such terminology is simply a reference to an examination of the evidence establishing Christianity as the one true religion of the one true God. Regardless of the source or nature of that evidence, however, the ultimate goal is to substantiate the existence of God, the inspiration of the Bible, the validity of the creation account found in Genesis 1-2, the deity and Sonship of Christ, and the essentiality of Christ's church.

Much of the evidence attending the truthfulness of Christianity can be examined within broad categories such as those listed above. But these do not tell the whole story, for within each major area of study there are important subcategories that offer additional insight. An illustration of this point would be a study of the inspiration of the Bible. It is possible to examine various arguments that establish the Bible as being God's inspired Word. Generally speaking, however, such a study may not examine such things as alleged internal contradictions, supposed historical inconsistencies, and other such matters. In order to respond to such charges, one must "dig a little deeper" into the evidence at hand.

The same is true of the evidence that establishes the existence of God. It is not a difficult task to assemble evidence that represents a compelling case for God's existence. Yet that evidence often may not touch on other equally important matters that have to do with God's personality and character (e.g., things like His eternality, His justice, His relationship to other members of the Godhead, etc.). Information on these topics must be derived from separate, independent studies.

Among the "subcategories" that Christian apologetics seeks to address in relation to God's existence are His nature and His interaction with man. It is not enough merely to acknowledge that God exists. Rather, it is necessary to know something about Him and what He expects from humankind. By necessity, then, any investigation into these matters eventually will have to address such topics as His mercy, His grace, His plan for mankind, etc.

It is my desire to examine those very subjects in this book. First, I would like to provide an in-depth look at God's mercy and grace. Second, I want to investigate the role of Christ as God's Son in His divine plan. Third, I intend to scrutinize man's estrangement from God and Heaven's remedy for that estrangement. And fourth, I plan to discuss the character and essentiality of Christ's divinely designed, blood-bought, Spirit-filled church. I invite you to join me as we study together these important subjects.

2

THE MERCY AND
GRACE OF GOD

The mercy and grace of God are at the core of one of the most
beautiful, yet one of the most heart-rending, accounts in all the Bible
—the story of Peter's denial of His Lord, and Jesus' reaction to that
denial. Christ had predicted that before His crucifixion Peter would deny Him three times (John 13:36-38). Peter did just that (John 18:25-
27). First, he was asked by a maid who controlled the door to the
court of the high priest if he was a disciple of Jesus. Peter denied that
he was. Second, he was asked by servants of the high priest if he was
indeed the Lord's disciple. Again, he denied knowing Jesus. Third,
he was asked if he was with the Lord when they arrested Him in the
Garden of Gethsemane. One last time, Peter vehemently denied the
Lord. The cock crowed, and the Lord looked across the courtyard.
As their eyes met, the text says simply that Peter "went out and wept
bitterly" (Luke 22:61-62).

When next we see Peter, he has given up. In fact, he said "I go a
fishing" (John 21:3). Peter's life as a follower of Christ was finished,
so far as he was concerned. He had decided to go back to his former
vocation. No doubt Peter felt that his sin against the Lord was so griev-
ous that even though he now believed the Lord to be risen, there

could be no further use for him in the kingdom. It was, then, to fishing that he would return.

It is a compliment to Peter's innate leadership ability that the other disciples followed him even on this sad occasion. As Peter and his friends fished one morning, the Lord appeared on the shore and called to them. When they brought the boat near, they saw that Christ had prepared a meal of fish and bread over an open fire. They sat, ate, and talked. As they did, the Lord asked Peter, "Simon, lovest thou me more than these?" (John 21:15). Peter assured Jesus that he did. But Christ appeared unsatisfied with Peter's response. He inquired a second time, and a third. After the last query, the text indicates that Peter was "grieved because Christ said unto him a third time, 'lovest thou me?' " (John 21:17).

Peter's uneasiness was saying, in essence, "What are you trying to do to me, Lord?" Jesus was asking: "Peter, can you comprehend —in spite of your denying heart—that I have forgiven you? Do you understand that the mercy and grace of God have been extended to you? There is still work for you to do. Go, use your immense talents in the advancement of the kingdom." Jesus loved Peter. And He wanted him back. Jesus simply was putting into action that which He had taught personally. Forgive, yes, even "70 times 7."

Perhaps during these events one of Christ's parables came to Peter's mind. He no doubt was familiar with the teaching of the Lord in Luke 7:36-50 (see the similar account found in Matthew 18:23-35). Jesus was eating with Simon, a Pharisee. Simon saw a worldly woman come into the Lord's presence, and thought: "This man, if he were a prophet, would have perceived who and what manner of woman this is that toucheth him, that she is a sinner" (Luke 7:39). Simon's point, of course, was that Christ should have driven away the sinful woman. But Jesus, knowing Simon's thoughts, presented a parable for his consideration.

Two servants owed their lord; one owed an enormous debt, and the other only a small amount. Yet the master forgave both of the debts. Jesus asked Simon: "Which of them therefore will love him the most?" (Luke 7:42). Simon correctly answered: "He, I suppose, to whom he forgave the most" (Luke 7:43). Jesus, through this parable, was saying to Simon: "I came here today and you would not even extend to me the common courtesy of washing my feet. This woman entered, cried, washed my feet with her tears, and dried them with her hair. I have forgiven her. She, therefore, should love me the most."

This woman had been a recipient of God's mercy and grace. She gratefully expressed devotion for the forgiveness offered by the Son of God. Simon, on the other hand, was too religious to beg, and too proud to accept it if offered. It is a sad but true fact that man will treat forgiveness lightly so long as he treats sin lightly. The worldly, fallen woman desperately desired the saving mercy and grace of God—and accepted it when it was extended. Christ's point to Simon was that man can appreciate **to what** he has been elevated (God's saving grace) only when he recognizes **from what** he has been saved (his own sinful state).

In this context, Christ's point to Peter becomes clear. "Peter, you denied me, not just once, but three times. Have I forgiven you? Yes, I have." Peter, too, had been the recipient of God's mercy and grace. He had much of which to be forgiven. Yet, **he had been forgiven**! The problem that relates to mercy and grace is not to be found in heaven; rather, it is to be found here on the Earth. Man often finds it difficult to accept God's mercy and grace. And often he finds it just as difficult to forgive himself. We do not stand in need of an accuser; God's law does that admirably, as the seventh chapter of Romans demonstrates. What we need is an Advocate (1 John 2:1-2)—someone to stand in our place, and to plead our case. We—laden with our burden of sin—have no right to stand before the majestic throne of God, even with the intent to beg for mercy. But Jesus the Righteous has that right. He made it clear to His disciples, and likewise has made it clear to us, that He is willing to be just such an Advocate on our behalf. The author of the book of Hebrews wrote:

Having then a great high priest, who hath passed through the heavens, Jesus the Son of God, let us hold fast our confession. For we have not a high priest that cannot be touched with the feeling of our infirmities; but one that hath been in all points tempted as we are, yet without sin (4:14-15).

The entire story of the Bible centers on man's need for mercy and grace. That story began in Genesis 3, and has been unfolding ever since. Fortunately, "the Lord is full of pity, and merciful" (James 5: 11). Even when Cain—a man who had murdered his own brother—begged for mercy, God heard his plea and placed a mark on him for his protection. God never has wanted to punish anyone. His words to that effect were recorded by Ezekiel: "Have I any pleasure in the death of the wicked? saith the Lord Jehovah; and not rather that he should return from his way, and live?... I have no pleasure in the death of him that dieth, saith the Lord Jehovah" (18:23,32). Similarly, in the times of Hosea sin was rampant. Life was barren. Worship to God had been polluted. The effects of Satan's rule were felt everywhere on the Earth. The Lord, suggested Hosea, "hath a controversy with the inhabitants of the land, because there is no truth, nor goodness, nor knowledge of God in the land" (4:1). Evidence of God's mercy and grace is seen, however, in the words spoken by Hosea on God's behalf:

How shall I give thee up, O Ephraim! How shall I cast thee off, Israel! ...my heart is turned within me, my compassions are kindled together. I will not execute the fierceness of mine anger, I will not return to destroy Ephraim; for I am God and not man; the Holy One in the midst of thee; and I will not come in wrath (11:8-9).

Solomon said that those who practice mercy and truth will find "favor and good understanding in the sight of God and man" (Proverbs 3:4). Many are those in the Bible who desperately sought the mercy and grace of God. Cain needed mercy and grace. Israel needed mercy and grace. Peter needed mercy and grace. And to all it was given, as God deemed appropriate. We must understand, however, several important facts about God's mercy and grace.

God is Sovereign in Delegating
His Mercy and Grace

First, we must realize that God is sovereign in granting both His mercy and His grace. When we speak of God's sovereign nature, it is a recognition on our part that whatever He wills is right. He alone determines the appropriate course of action; He acts and speaks at the whim of no outside force, including mankind.

When humans become the recipients of heaven's grace, the unfathomable has happened. The apostle Paul wrote: "For all have sinned, and fall short of the glory of God.... For the wages of sin is death; but the free gift of God is eternal life in Christ Jesus our Lord" (Romans 3:23; 6:23). God—our Justifiable Accuser—has become our Vindicator. He has extended to us His wonderful love, as expressed by His mercy and His grace.

Mercy has been defined as feeling "sympathy with the misery of another, and especially sympathy manifested in act" (Vine, 1940, 3: 61). Mercy is more than just sympathetic feelings. It is sympathy in concert with action. Grace often has been defined as the "unmerited favor of God." If grace is unmerited, then none can claim it as an unalienable right. If grace is undeserved, then none is entitled to it. If grace is a gift, then none can demand it. Grace is the antithesis of justice. After God's grace has been meted out, there remains only divine justice. Because salvation is through grace (Ephesians 2:8-9), the very chief of sinners is not beyond the reach of divine grace. Because salvation is by grace, boasting is excluded and God receives the glory.

When justice is meted out, we **receive what we deserve**. When mercy is extended, we **do not receive what we deserve**. When grace is bestowed, we **receive what we do not deserve**.

Perhaps no one could appreciate this better than Peter. It was he who said: "And if the righteous is scarcely saved, where shall the ungodly and sinner appear?" (1 Peter 4:18). Paul reminded the first-century Christians in Rome that "scarcely for a righteous man will one die: for peradventure for the good man some one would even dare to die. But God commendeth his own love toward us, in that, while we were yet sinners, Christ died for us" (Romans 5:7-8).

Yet because it is a free gift, and unearned, it remains within God's sovereign right to bestow it as He sees fit. A beautiful expression of this fact can be seen in the prayers of two men who found themselves in similar circumstances—in that both were under the sentence of death. In Numbers 20, the story is told of God's commanding Moses to speak to the rock in the wilderness, so that it would yield water for the Israelites. Rather than obey the command of God to speak to the rock, however, Moses struck it instead. The Lord said to him: "Because ye believed not in me, to sanctify me in the eyes of the children of Israel, therefore ye shall not bring this assembly into the land which I have given them" (Numbers 20:12). Years later, God called Moses to the top of Mount Nebo and allowed him to look across into the promised land, but He vowed that Moses would not enter into Canaan with the Israelites. Moses begged God to permit him to go (Deuteronomy 3:26), but his plea was denied.

Yet king Hezekiah, likewise under a sentence of death, petitioned God to let him live, and God added 15 years to his life. Moses wrote: "The Lord would not hear me," and died. But to Hezekiah it was said: "I have heard thy prayer" (2 Kings 20:1-6), and his life was spared. What a beautiful illustration and amplification of Romans 9:15: "For he saith unto Moses, I will have mercy on whom I have mercy, and I will have compassion on whom I have compassion." God is sovereign in His mercy and His grace.

God's Grace Does Not Mean a Lack of Consequences to Sin

Second, we must recognize that God's granting mercy and grace does not somehow negate the consequences of sin here and now. While mercy may ensue, so may sin's consequences. Perhaps the most touching story in the Bible illustrating this eternal truth is the account of king David. How could a man of David's faith and righteousness commit the terrible sins attributed to him? David was about 50 years old at the time. Fame and fortune were his as Israel's popular, beloved king. He had taken his vows before God (see Psalm 101). He had insisted on righteousness in his nation. The people had been taught to love, respect, and honor the God of heaven. David, their king, also was their example. He was a man after God's own heart (1 Samuel 13:14).

But he committed the sin of adultery with Bathsheba (2 Samuel 11-12), and then had her husband, Uriah, murdered. One cannot help but be reminded of the sin of Achan (Joshua 7) when he took booty from a war and hid it under the floor of his tent after the Israelites were commanded specifically not to take any such items. Achan said, "I saw..., I coveted..., I took..., I hid..." (Joshua 7:21). Is that not what King David did? But Achan and David also could state, "I paid." Achan paid with his life; David paid with twenty years of heartbreak, strife, and the loss of a child that meant everything to him.

The prophet Nathan was sent by God to the great king. He told David the story of a rich man who had many sheep in his flock, and of a poor man who had but one small ewe that practically was part of the family. When a visitor appeared at the rich man's door, the rich man took the single ewe owned by the poor man and slaughtered it for the visitor's meal. Upon hearing what had happened, David was overwhelmed with anger and vowed, "As Jehovah liveth, the man that hath done this is worthy to die" (2 Samuel 12:5).

Nathan looked the powerful king in the eye and said, "Thou art the man" (2 Samuel 12:7). The enormity of David's sin swept over him and he said, "I have sinned" (2 Samuel 12:13). David, even through his sin, was a man who loved righteousness. Now that Nathan had shown him his sin, he felt a repulsion which demanded a cleansing that could come only from God. His description of the consequences of sin on the human heart is one of the most vivid in all of Scripture, and should move each of us deeply. His agonizing prayer is recorded in Psalm 51. David cried out: "Have mercy upon me, O God, according to thy lovingkindness."

David needed a new heart; sin had defiled his old one. He likewise realized that he needed to undergo an inner renewal; pride and lust had destroyed his spirit. So, David prayed for a proper spirit. He could do nothing but cast himself on the mercy and grace of God. David laid on the altar his own sinful heart and begged God to cleanse, recreate, and restore his life. God did forgive. He did cleanse. He did recreate. He did restore.

But the consequences of David's sin remained. The child growing in Bathsheba's womb died after birth. In addition, the prophet Nathan made it clear to David that "the sword shall never depart from thy house," and that God would "raise up evil against thee out of thine own house" (2 Samuel 12:10-11). David's life never again would be the same. His child was dead, his reputation was damaged, his influence was all but destroyed.

David learned that the penalty for personal sin often is felt in the lives of others as well. He prayed that those who loved and served the Lord would not have to bear his shame, but such was not to be. The shame of the one is the shame of the many; as God's people, we are bound together. More often than not, what affects one of us affects all of us.

It is to David's credit that once his sin was uncovered, he did not try to deny it. Solomon, his son, later would write: "He that covereth his transgressions shall not prosper; but whoso confesseth and forsaketh them shall obtain mercy" (Proverbs 28:13).

Mercy and Grace Are Expensive

Third, we should realize that the mercy and grace God uses to cover mankind's sins are not cheap. They cost heaven its finest jewel —the Son of God. The popular, old song says it well:

I owed a debt I could not pay
He paid a debt He did not owe
I needed someone to wash my sins away.
So now I sing a brand new song—amazing grace
Christ paid the debt I could never pay.

Jesus' death represented His total commitment to us. Isaiah prophesied:

> Surely he hath borne our griefs, and carried our sorrows; yet we did esteem him stricken, smitten of God, and afflicted. But he was wounded for our transgressions, he was bruised for our iniquities; the chastisement of our peace was upon him; and with his stripes we are healed. All we like sheep have gone astray; we have turned everyone to his own way; and Jehovah hath laid on him the iniquity of us all.... He bare the sin of many, and made intercession for the transgressors (53:4-6, 12).

Paul wrote: "Him who knew no sin he made to be sin on our behalf that we might become the righteousness of God in him" (2 Corinthians 5:21).

Grace does not **eliminate** human responsibility; rather, grace **emphasizes** human responsibility. Grace, because it cost God so much, delivers agonizing duties and obligations. It is seemingly a great paradox that Christianity is free, yet at the same time is so very costly. Jesus warned: "If any man will come after me, let him deny himself, and take up his cross, and follow me" (Matthew 16:24). Paul summarized it like this: "I have been crucified with Christ; and it is no longer I that live, but Christ liveth in me: and that life which I now live in the flesh I live in faith, the faith which is in the Son of God, who loved me, and gave himself up for me. I do not make void the grace of God" (Galatians 2:20-21).

Grace does not make one **irresponsible**; rather, it makes one **more responsible**! Paul asked: "What shall we say then? Shall we continue in sin, that grace may abound? God forbid" (Romans 6:1-2). God's grace is accessed through willful obedience to the "perfect law of liberty" (James 1:25). It is God's law that informs us of the availability of grace, of the manner in which we appropriate it, and of the blessings that stem from living within it.

The testimony of Scripture is abundantly clear when it speaks of the importance of the "obedience of faith" (Romans 1:5). We are to be obedient to God by returning to Him from an alien, sinful state, and, once redeemed, through our continued faithfulness as evinced by our works. Grace and works of obedience are not mutually exclusive.

Neither are grace and law mutually exclusive, as some today have suggested. One who is "in Christ" does not live under the dominion of sin, since Christianity is a system of grace. The apostle to the Gentiles stated: "Ye are not under the law, but under grace" (Romans 6:14). He cannot mean that we are under no law at all, because in the following verses he spoke of early Christians being "obedient from the heart to that form of teaching" delivered to them (6:17). These Christians had obeyed God's law, and were living faithfully under that law. They understood that "faith worketh by love" (Galatians 5:6). The terms "law," "works," and "grace" are not at odds, but like all things within God's plan, exist in perfect harmony.

We Are Saved Through Grace

Fourth, let us remember that our salvation is by atonement, not attainment. Because salvation is a free gift (Romans 6:23), man never can earn it. Unmerited favor cannot be merited! God did for us what we, on our own, could not do. Jesus paid the price we could not pay. From beginning to end, the scheme of redemption—including all that God has done, is doing, and will do—is one continuous act of grace. The Scriptures speak of God "reconciling the world unto himself, not reckoning unto them their trespasses, and having committed unto us the word of reconciliation" (2 Corinthians 5:19). Peter stated:

> Knowing that ye were redeemed, not with corruptible things, with silver or gold, from your vain manner of life handed down from your fathers; but with precious blood, as of a lamb without blemish and without spot, even the blood of Christ (1 Peter 1:18-19).

God has promised mercy and grace to those who believe on His Son (John 3:16), repent of their sins (Luke 13:3), and have those sins remitted through baptism (Acts 2:38; 22:16). Subsequent to the Day of Pentecost, Peter called upon his audiences to: "Repent ye therefore, and turn again, that your sins may be blotted out" (Acts 3:19). The word for "blotted out" derives from the Greek word meaning to "wipe out, erase, or obliterate." The New Testament uses the word to refer to "blotting out" the old law (Colossians 2:14) and to "blotting out" a person's name from the Book of Life (Revelation 3: 5). One of the great prophetical utterances of the Old Testament was that "their sin will I remember no more" (Jeremiah 31:34).

Our sins were borne by Jesus on the cross. He paid our debt so that we, like undeserving Barabbas, might be set free. In this way, God could be just, and at the same time Justifier of those who believe in and obey His Son. By refusing to extend mercy to Jesus on the cross, God was able to extend mercy to me—**if** I submit in obedience to His commands.

There was no happy solution to the justice/mercy dilemma. There was no way that God could remain just (since justice demands that the wages of sin be paid) and yet save His Son from death. Christ was abandoned to the cross so that mercy could be extended to sinners who stood condemned (Galatians 3:10). God could not save sinners by fiat—upon the ground of mere authority alone—without violating His own attribute of divine justice. Paul discussed God's response to this problem in Romans 3:24-26:

> Being justified freely by his grace through the redemption that is in Christ Jesus; whom God set forth to be a propitiation, through faith, in his blood...for the showing of his righteousness...that he might himself be just and the justifier of him that hath faith in Jesus.

Man's salvation was no arbitrary arrangement. God did not decide merely to consider man a sinner, and then determine to save him upon a principle of mercy. Sin placed man in a state of antagonism toward God. Sinners are condemned because they have violated God's law, and because God's justice cannot permit Him to ignore sin. Sin could be forgiven only as a result of the vicarious death of God's Son. Because sinners are redeemed by the sacrifice of Christ, and not their own righteousness, they are sanctified by the mercy and grace of God.

Our Response to Mercy and Grace

What, then, should be our response to mercy and grace? (1) Let us remember that "blessed are the merciful, for they shall obtain mercy" (Matthew 5:7). It is a biblical principle that unless we extend mercy, we cannot obtain mercy. Jesus taught: "For if ye forgive men their trespasses, your heavenly Father will also forgive you; but if ye forgive not men their trespasses, neither will your Father forgive your trespasses" (Matthew 6:14-15). We would do well to recall the adage that "he who cannot forgive destroys the bridge over which he, too, one day must pass." If we expect to be forgiven, then let us be prepared to forgive.

(2) Let us remember that mercy and grace demand action on our part. Mercy is to feel "sympathy with the misery of another, and especially sympathy manifested in act." Luke recorded an example of Christ's mercy in healing ten lepers who "lifted up their voices saying, 'Jesus, Master, have mercy on us' " (Luke 17:13). Did these diseased and dying men want merely a few kind words uttered in their direction? Hardly. They wanted to be healed! When the publican prayed so penitently, "God, be thou merciful to me a sinner" (Luke 18:13), he was asking for more than tender feelings of compassion. He wanted something done about his pitiful condition. Mercy and grace are compassion in action.

(3) Let us remember that nothing must take precedence over our Savior. If we have to choose between Christ and a friend, spouse, or child, Christ comes first. He demands no less (Luke 4:25-35)—but His demands are consistent with His sufferings on our behalf. He insists that we take up our cross: He took up His. He insists that we lose our life to find it: He lost His. He insists that we give up our families for His sake: He gave up His for ours. He demands that we give up everything for Him: He had nowhere to lay His head, and His only possession—the robe on His back—was taken from Him. Yes, the costs sometimes are high; but the blessings that we receive in return are priceless. He dispenses mercy and grace, and offers eternal salvation to all those who will believe in and obey Him.

Conclusion

In Luke 15, Jesus spoke of a wayward son who had sinned against his father and squandered his precious inheritance. Upon returning home, he decided to say to his father: "Make me as one of thy hired servants" (15:19). He was prepared for the worst.

But he received the best. His father, "while he was yet afar off, ...was moved with compassion, and ran, and fell on his neck, and kissed him" (Luke 15:20). The son did not receive what he **deserved**; he received **what he did not deserve**. He received mercy and grace. His father wanted him back!

Does our heavenly Father want us back? Oh, yes! Paul wrote: "For ye were bought with a price" (1 Corinthians 6:20). Let us yearn for the day when we can stand before His throne and thank Him for granting us mercy and grace—and for paying the debt we could not pay, and the debt He did not owe.

3

JESUS CHRIST—
LORD AND SAVIOR

On Tuesday, prior to the Christ's crucifixion the following Friday, Jesus engaged in a discussion with the Pharisees, who made no secret of their hatred for Him. When Matthew recorded the scene in his Gospel, he first commented on an earlier skirmish the Lord had with the Sadducees: "But the Pharisees, when they heard that he had put the Sadducees to silence, gathered themselves together" (22:34).

Jesus—with penetrating logic and an incomparable knowledge of the Old Testament Scriptures—had routed the Sadducees completely. No doubt the Pharisees thought they could do better. Yet they were about to endure the same embarrassing treatment.

In the midst of His discussion with the Pharisees, Jesus asked: "What think ye of the Christ? Whose son is he?" (Matthew 22:42). They were unable to answer the questions satisfactorily because their hypocrisy prevented them from comprehending both Jesus' nature and His mission. The questions the Lord asked on that day, however, are ones that every rational, sane person must answer eventually.

The two questions were intended to raise the matter of Christ's deity. The answers—had the Pharisees' spiritual myopia not prevented them from responding correctly—were intended to confirm it. Today, these questions still raise the spectre of Christ's identity. Who is Jesus? Is He, as He claimed to be, the Son of God? Was He, as many around Him claimed, God incarnate? Is He, as the word "deity" implies, of divine nature and rank?

Christ as a Historical Figure

The series of events that would lead to Jesus' becoming the world's best-known historical figure began in first-century Palestine. There are four primary indicators of this fact. First, when Daniel was asked by king Nebuchadnezzar to interpret his wildly imaginative dream, the prophet revealed that God would establish the Messianic kingdom during the time of the Roman Empire (viz., the fourth kingdom represented in the king's dream; see Daniel 2:24-45). Roman domination of Palestine began in 63 B.C., and continued until A.D. 476.

Second, the Christ was promised to come before "the scepter" departed from Judah (Genesis 49:10). Bible students recognize that this prophecy has reference to the Messiah ("Shiloh") arriving before the Jews lost their national sovereignty and judicial power (the "scepter" of Genesis 49). Thus, Christ had to have come prior to the Jews' losing their power to execute capital punishment (John 18:31). When Rome deposed Archelaus in A.D. 6, Coponius was installed as Judea's first procurator. Interestingly, "the...procurator held the power of jurisdiction with regard to capital punishment" (Solomon, 1972, 13:117). Hence, Christ was predicted to come sometime prior to A.D. 6 (see also McDowell, 1972, pp. 176-178).

Third, Daniel predicted that the Messiah would bring an end to "sacrifice and offering" before the destruction of Jerusalem (cf. Daniel 9:24-27 and Matthew 24:15; see also Jackson, 1997a). History records that the Temple was obliterated by the Romans in A.D. 70.

Fourth, the Messiah was to be born in Bethlehem of Judea (Micah 5:2). It also is a matter of record that Jesus was born in Bethlehem while Palestine was under Roman rule, before Judah lost her judicial power, and before the destruction of Jerusalem (see also Matthew 2:3-6; Luke 2:2-6).

Christ in the Old Testament

The Old and New Testaments portray a portrait of Christ that presents valuable evidence for the person desiring to answer the questions, "What think ye of the Christ?," and "Whose son is he?" In Isaiah 7:14, for example, the prophet declared that a virgin would conceive, bear a son, and name him "Immanuel," which means "God with us" (a prophecy that was fulfilled in the birth of Christ; Matthew 1:22-23). Later, Isaiah referred to this son as "Mighty God" (9:6). In fact, in the year that king Uzziah died, Isaiah said he saw "the Lord" sitting upon a throne (see Isaiah 6:1ff.). Overpowered by the scene, God's servant exclaimed: "Woe is me,...for mine eyes have seen the King, Jehovah of hosts" (6:5). In the New Testament, John wrote: "These things said Isaiah, because he saw His [Christ's] glory; and he spake of him" (John 12:41).

Isaiah urged God's people to sanctify "Jehovah of hosts" (8:12-14), a command applied to Jesus by Peter (1 Peter 3:14-15). Furthermore, Isaiah's "Jehovah" was to become a stone of stumbling and a rock of offense (8:14), a description that New Testament writers applied to Christ (cf. Romans 9:33, 1 Peter 2:8). Isaiah foretold that John the Baptizer would prepare the way for the coming of **Jehovah** (40:3). It is well known that John was the forerunner of **Christ** (cf. Matthew 3:3, John 1:23).

Isaiah pictured Christ not only as a silent "lamb" (53:7), but as a man Who "a bruised reed will he not break, and a dimly burning wick will he not quench" (42:3; cf. Matthew 12:20). J.W. McGarvey explained the imagery in these verses as follows:

A bruised reed, barely strong enough to stand erect...a smoking flax (a lamp wick), its flame extinguished and its fire almost gone, fitly represent the sick, and lame, and blind who were brought to Jesus to be healed. ...he would heal their bruises and fan their dying energies into a flame (1875, p. 106).

Other Old Testament writers illuminated Christ in their writings as well. The psalmist suggested He would be known as zealous for righteousness (Psalm 69:9), that He would be hated without cause (Psalm 22), and that He would triumph over death (Psalm 16:8-11). Daniel referred to His coming kingdom as one that would "stand forever" (12:44). The prophets' portrait of Christ was intended not only to foreshadow His coming, but to make Him all the more visible to the people in New Testament times as well (see Bromling, 1991b)s.

Christ in the New Testament

The New Testament is equally explicit in its commentary regarding the Christ, and offers extensive corroboration of the Old Testament declarations concerning Him. The prophets had portrayed the Messiah's demise as unjust, painful, and vicarious (Isaiah 53:4-6; Psalm 22). In the New Testament, Paul reiterated that fact (Romans 5:6-8). The prophets predicted that He would be betrayed by a friend (Psalm 41:9) for a mere thirty pieces of silver (Zechariah 11:12), and He was (Luke 22:47-48; Matthew 26:15). They said that He would be mocked (Psalm 22:7-8), spat upon (Isaiah 50:6), numbered among common criminals (Isaiah 53:12), pierced through (Zechariah 12:10), and forsaken by God (cf. Psalm 22:1), and He was (Luke 23:35; Matthew 26:67; Matthew 27:46; Mark 15:27-28; John 19:37; John 20:25; Mark 15:34). Without any explanation, an inspired prophet predicted that the suffering servant's hands and feet would be pierced (Psalm 22:16). Later revelation reveals the reason for such a statement: He was nailed to a cross (Luke 23:33).

The prophets had said that He would be raised from the dead so that He could sit upon the throne of David (Isaiah 9:7). This occurred, as Peter attested in his sermon on Pentecost following the resurrection (Acts 2:30). He would rule, not Judah, but the most powerful kingdom ever known. As King, Christ was to rule (from heaven) the kingdom that "shall never be destroyed" and that "shall break in pieces and consume all these [earthly] kingdoms, and...shall stand forever" (Daniel 2:44). The New Testament establishes the legitimacy of His kingdom (Colossians 1:13; 1 Corinthians 15:24-25). The subjects of this royal realm were to be from every nation on Earth (Isaiah 2:2), and were prophesied to enjoy a life of peace and harmony that ignores any and all human distinctions, prejudices, or biases (cf. Isaiah 2:4 and Galatians 3:28). This King would be arrayed, not in the regal purple of a carnal king, but in the humble garments of a holy priest (Psalm 110:4; Hebrews 5:6). Like Melchizedek, the Messiah was to be both Priest and King (Genesis 14:18), guaranteeing that His subjects could approach God without the interference of a clergy class. Instead, as the New Testament affirms, Christians offer their petitions directly to God through their King—Who mediates on their behalf (cf. Matthew 6:9; John 14:13-14; 1 Timothy 2:5; Hebrews 10: 12,19-22). It would be impossible for the New Testament writers to provide any clearer answers than they did to the questions that Christ asked the Pharisees.

Christ as a Man

The Scriptures teach that Jesus possessed two natures—divine and human. As an eternal Being (Isaiah 9:6; Micah 5:2; John 1:1ff.), He was God; yet, He became man (1 Timothy 2:5), made in the likeness of sinful flesh (Romans 8:3), though without sin (Hebrews 4:15). Isaiah observed that Christ would be "a **man** of sorrows, and acquainted with grief" Who would **grow up** "as a tender plant, and as a root out of dry ground" (Isaiah 53:2-3).

As a human, the prophets had said, Christ was to be the seed of woman (Genesis 3:15), and a descendant of Abraham, Isaac, Jacob, and David (Genesis 22:18; 26:4; 28:14; 2 Samuel 7:12-13). The New Testament confirms that He was born of a woman (Galatians

4:4) who was a virgin (Matthew 1:23), and that He was the descendant of Abraham, Isaac, Jacob, and David (Matthew 1:1ff.). The apostle John stated that He had become flesh and had dwelt among men (John 1:14). Paul wrote that Christ was recognized "in fashion as a man" (Philippians 2:7-8). From his position as a physician, Luke wrote that Christ "advanced in wisdom and stature, and in favor with God and men" (Luke 2:52). He was able to learn (Hebrews 5:8). He experienced hunger (Matthew 4:2), thirst (John 19:28), weariness (John 4:6), anger (Mark 3:5), frustration (Mark 9:19), joy (John 15:11), sadness (John 11:35), and grief (Luke 19:41; Hebrews 5:7). He was "in all points tempted as we are, yet without sin" (Hebrews 4:15). But most significantly, He was able to die (Mark 15:44). In every respect, He was as human as you and I, which is why He could, and did, refer to Himself as the "Son of Man" (see Matthew 1:20; 9:6; et al.).

But the impact He had on the world was not due to His physical appearance. In fact, Isaiah foretold that He would have "no form nor comeliness; and when we see Him, there is no beauty that we should desire Him" (Isaiah 53:2). Rather, it was His nature and His character that made Him so intriguing, so commanding a figure, and so worthy of honor, respect, and worship. Here we see a man—but no mere man, for He is the only man ever to be born of a virgin (Isaiah 7:14; Matthew 1:18), and to whom the inspired prophets dared to apply the revered name of "Jehovah" (Isaiah 40:3).

Why do the Scriptures place importance upon the **human** nature of Christ? Wayne Jackson has suggested:

> If Christ had not become a man, He could not have died. Deity, as pure Spirit-essence, possesses **immortality** (1 Tim. 6:16—the Greek word denotes deathlessness). The writer of Hebrews makes it wonderfully plain that Christ partook of "flesh and blood" that "through death he might bring to nought him that had the power of death, that is, the devil" (Heb. 2:14). If Christ had not died, there would have been no atonement, no forgiveness of sins—the human family would have been hopelessly lost forever! Thank God for Christ's humanity (1979, p. 66, emp. in orig.).

Christ as God

The Scriptures do not speak of Christ as **just** a man, however. They also acknowledge His divine nature. In most of its occurrences, "Jehovah" is applied to the first person of the Godhead (i.e., the Father—Matthew 28:19). For example: "Jehovah said unto my Lord, Sit thou at my right hand, until I make thine enemies thy footstool" (Psalm 110:1). Jesus later explained that this verse pictures the Father addressing the Christ (Luke 20:42).

Yet the name "Jehovah" also is used on occasion to refer to Christ. For example, Isaiah prophesied concerning the mission of John the Baptizer: "The voice of one that crieth, Prepare ye in the wilderness the way of Jehovah; make level in the desert a highway for our God" (Isaiah 40:3; cf. Matthew 3:3, Mark 1:3, Luke 3:4). John was sent to prepare the way for Jesus Christ (John 1:29-34). But Isaiah said that John would prepare the way of **Jehovah**. Clearly, Jesus and Jehovah are the same.

The writer of Hebrews quoted the Father as addressing His Son in this way: "Thou, Lord [Jehovah—Psalm 102:25], in the beginning did lay the foundation of the earth, and the heavens are the works of thy hands" (Hebrews 1:10). This verse not only applies the word "Jehovah" to Jesus, but actually attributes the quotation **to the mouth of God**. Again, Jesus and Jehovah are used synonymously (see Bromling, 1991a).

Furthermore, Jesus spoke and acted like God. He affirmed that He was "one" with the Father (John 10:30). He forgave sins—a prerogative of God alone (Mark 2:5,7). He accepted the worship of men (John 9:38) which is due only to God (Matthew 4:10), and which good angels (Revelation 22:8-9) and good men (Matthew 4:10) refuse.

In addition, Jesus plainly is called "God" a number of times within the New Testament. In John 1:1, regarding Him Who became flesh and dwelt among men (1:14), the Bible says: "the Word was God." And in John 20:28, one of the disciples, Thomas, upon being confronted with empirical evidence for the Lord's resurrection, proclaimed: "My Lord and my God!" Significantly, and appropriately, Christ accepted the designation. Additional passages that reveal Christ as God include Philippians 2:5ff., 2 Corinthians 4:4, Colossians 1:15, and many others.

Choices Regarding Christ's Deity

When Jesus was put on trial before the Sanhedrin, the Jewish high priest asked: "Are you the Christ, the Son of the Blessed?" To that question Christ replied simply, "I am" (Mark 14:62). In view of the exalted nature of such a claim, and its ultimate end results, there are but three possible views one may entertain in reference to Christ's claim of being deity: (1) He was a liar and con-artist; (2) He was a madman; or (3) He was exactly Who He said He was.

In his book, *Evidence that Demands a Verdict*, Josh McDowell titled one chapter: "The Trilemma—Lord, Liar, or Lunatic?" His purpose was to point out that, considering the grandiose nature of Christ's claims, He was either a liar, a lunatic, or the Lord. McDowell introduced his chapter on Christ's deity with a quotation from the famous British apologist of Cambridge University, C.S. Lewis, who wrote:

> I am trying here to prevent anyone saying the really foolish thing that people often say about Him: "I'm ready to accept Jesus as a great moral teacher, but I don't accept His claim to be God." That is the one thing we must not say. A man who was merely a man and said the sort of things Jesus said would not be a great moral teacher. He would either be a lunatic—on a level with the man who says he is a poached egg—or else he would be the Devil of Hell. You must make your choice. Either this man was, and is, the Son of God: or else a madman or something worse. You can shut Him up for a fool, you can spit at Him and kill Him as a demon; or you can fall at His feet and call Him Lord and God. But let us not come up with any patronising nonsense about His being a great human teacher. He has not left that open to us. He did not intend to (1952, pp. 40-41).

Was Christ a Liar?

Was Christ a liar? A charlatan? A "messianic manipulator"? Hugh J. Schonfield, in *The Passover Plot*, claimed that He was all three. Schonfield suggested that Jesus manipulated His life in such a way as to counterfeit the events described in the Old Testament prophecies about the Messiah. At times, this required "contriving those events when necessary, contending with friends and foes to ensure that the predictions would be fulfilled" (1965, p. 7). Schonfield charged that Jesus "plotted and schemed with the utmost skill and resourcefulness, sometimes making secret arrangements, taking advantage of every circumstance conducive to the attainment of his objectives" (p. 155). He further asserted that Jesus even planned to fake His own death on the cross. Unfortunately, however, Jesus had not counted on having a Roman soldier pierce His side with a spear. Thus, instead of recovering from His stupor, Jesus died unexpectedly. On Saturday night, His body was moved to a secret place so that His tomb would be empty on the next day, thus leaving the impression of His resurrection and, simultaneously, His deity (pp. 161,165). One writer has asked, however:

> But does this reconstruction of the life of Christ ring true? Even if a charlatan **could** beguile a few followers into believing that he had fulfilled a few of the prophecies (either by coincidence, or by contrivance), how could he possibly fulfill those which were beyond his control? How could an impostor have planned his betrayal price? How could he have known the money would be used to buy the potter's field (cf. Zechariah 11:13, Matthew 27:7)? How could he have known that men would gamble for his clothing (cf. Psalm 22:17-18, Matthew 27:35-36)? Yet, these are just a few of the prophecies over which he would have no control. Jesus fulfilled every single one of them (Bromling, 1991b, 11:47).

In considering the possibility that Christ was little more than an accomplished liar, renowned biblical historian Philip Schaff wrote:

> How in the name of logic, common sense, and experience, could an impostor that is a deceitful, selfish, depraved man—

have invented, and consistently maintained from the beginning to end, the purest and noblest character known in history with the most perfect air of truth and reality? How could he have conceived and successfully carried out a plan of unparalleled beneficence, moral magnitude, and sublimity, and sacrificed his own life for it, in the face of the strongest prejudices of his people and ages? (1913, pp. 94-95).

Further, the question must be asked: What sane man would be willing to **die** for what he **knows** is a lie? As McDowell summarized the matter: "Someone who lived as Jesus lived, taught as Jesus taught, and died as Jesus died could not have been a liar" (1972, p. 106).

Was Christ a Lunatic?

Was Jesus merely a psychotic lunatic Who sincerely (albeit mistakenly) viewed Himself as God incarnate? Such a view rarely has been entertained by anyone cognizant of Christ's life and teachings. Schaff inquired:

Is such an intellect—clear as the sky, bracing as the mountain air, sharp and penetrating as a sword, thoroughly healthy and vigorous, always ready and always self-possessed—liable to a radical and most serious delusion concerning His own character and mission? Preposterous imagination! (1913, pp. 97-98).

Would a raving lunatic teach that we should do unto others as we would have them do unto us? Would a lunatic teach that we should pray for our enemies? Would a lunatic teach that we should "turn the other cheek," and then set an example of exactly how to do that—even unto death? Would a lunatic present an ethical/moral code like the one found within the text of the Sermon on the Mount? Hardly! Lunacy of the sort ascribed to Christ by His detractors does not produce such genius. Schaff wrote:

Self-deception in a matter so momentous, and with an intellect in all respects so clear and so sound, is equally out of the question. How could He be an enthusiast or a madman who never lost the even balance of His mind, who sailed serenely over all the troubles and persecutions, as the sun above the clouds, who always returned the wisest answer to tempting questions, who calmly and deliberately predicted His death on the cross, His resurrection on the third day, the outpouring of the Holy Spirit, the founding of His Church, the destruction of Jerusalem—predictions which have been literally fulfilled? A character so original, so completely, so uniformly consistent, so perfect, so human and yet so high above all human greatness, can be neither a fraud nor a fiction. The poet, as has been well said, would be in this case greater than the hero. It would take more than a Jesus to invent a Jesus (1910, p. 109).

Was Christ Deity?

If Jesus was not a liar or a lunatic, then the questions Jesus asked the Pharisees still remain: "What think ye of the Christ? Whose son is He?" Was Jesus, in fact, exactly Who He claimed to be? Was He God incarnate? The evidence suggests that, indeed, He was.

Evidence for the Deity of Christ

In Mark 10, an account is recorded concerning a rich young ruler who, in speaking to Christ, addressed Him as "Good Teacher." Upon hearing this reference, Jesus asked the man: "Why callest thou me good? None is good, save one, even God" (Mark 10:17).

Was Christ suggesting that His countryman's loyalty was misplaced, and that He was unworthy of being called "good" (in the sense that ultimately only God merits such a designation)? No. In fact, Christ was suggesting that He **was worthy** of the appellation. He wanted the ruler to understand the significance of the title he had used. R.C. Foster paraphrased Jesus' response as follows: "Do you know the meaning of this word you apply to me and which you use so freely? There is none good save God; if you apply that term to me, and you understand what you mean, you affirm that I am God" (1971, p. 1022).

What evidence establishes Christ's deity? Among other things, it includes Christ's fulfillment of Old Testament prophecies, His confirmation of His Sonship via the miracles He performed, His crucifixion and subsequent resurrection, and His post-resurrection appearances.

Fulfillment of Old Testament Prophecies

Scholars have documented over 300 messianic prophecies in the Old Testament (Lockyer, 1973, p. 21). From Genesis through Malachi, the history of Jesus is foretold in minute detail. Bible critics who wish to disprove Christ's deity, must refute fulfilled prophecy. To accomplish this, one would have to contend that Jesus did not fulfill the prophecies **genuinely**; rather, He only **appeared** to fulfill them. Yet with over 300 prophecies relating to Christ—none of which can be dismissed flippantly—this is an impossible task (see Bromling, 1989). Could Christ have fulfilled 300+ prophetic utterances **by chance**? P.W. Stoner and R.C. Newman selected eight specific prophecies and then calculated the probability of one man fulfilling only those eight. Their conclusion was that 1 man in 10^{17} could do it (1971, p. 106). The probability that a single man could fulfill—by chance—**all** of the prophecies relating to Christ and His ministry would be practically incalculable, and the idea that a single man did so would be utterly absurd.

Performance of Genuine Miracles

Christ also backed up His claims by working miracles. Throughout history, God had empowered other people to perform miracles. But while their miracles confirmed they were **servants** of God, Jesus' miracles were intended to prove that He **is** God (John 10:37-38; cf. John 20:30-31).

While in prison, John the Baptizer sent his followers to ask Jesus: "Art thou he that cometh, or look we for another?" (Matthew 11:3). Jesus' response was: "Go and tell John...the blind receive their sight and the lame walk, the lepers are cleansed, and the deaf hear, and the dead are raised up, and the poor have good tidings preached to them" (Matthew 11:4-5). "Over seven hundred years earlier, the prophet Isaiah predicted that those very things would be done by the Messiah (Isaiah 35:5-6; 61:1). Jesus wasn't merely saying, 'Look at all the good things I am doing.' He was saying: 'I am doing **exactly what the Coming One is supposed to do!**'" (Bromling, 1995, 15: 19, emp. added).

When Peter addressed the very people who had put Jesus to death, he reminded them that Christ's unique identity had been proved "by mighty works and wonders and signs which God did by him in the midst of you, even as ye yourselves know" (Acts 2:22). The key phrase here is "even as ye yourselves know." The Jews had witnessed Christ's miracles occurring among them on practically a daily basis. And, unlike the pseudo-miracles allegedly performed by today's "spiritualists," Jesus' miracles were feats that truly defied naturalistic explanation. In the presence of many witnesses, the Nazarene not only gave sight to the blind, healed lepers, fed thousands from a handful of food, and made the lame to walk, but also calmed turbulent seas and raised the dead! Although not overly eager to admit it, Jesus' critics often were brought face-to-face with the truth that no one could do what Jesus did unless God was with Him (John 3:2; see also John 9).

The Resurrection, and Post-Resurrection Appearances

Likely, however, the most impressive miracle involving Jesus was His resurrection. In agreement with Old Testament prophecy, and just as He had promised, Christ came forth from the tomb three days after His brutal crucifixion (Matthew 16:21; 27:63; 28:1-8). His resurrection was witnessed by soldiers who had been appointed to guard His tomb. In the end, these soldiers had to be bribed to change their story, so that the Jewish leaders would not lose credibility, and to prevent the Jewish people from recognizing their true Messiah (Matthew 28:11-15). It is a matter of history that Christ's tomb was empty on that Sunday morning almost 2,000 years ago. If Jesus were not raised from the dead, how came His guarded and sealed tomb to be empty?

That Christ had been raised from the dead was witnessed by many different types of people: the soldiers who guarded His tomb; the women who came early in the morning to anoint Him with spices; eleven apostles; and more than 500 other witnesses (1 Corinthians 15:4-8). When they saw the living, breathing Jesus—days after His death—they had concrete proof that He was Who He claimed to be all along! Even his detractors could not deny successfully the fact, and significance, of the empty tomb.

Thousands of people go annually to the graves of the founders of the Buddhist and Muslim religions to pay homage. Yet Christians do not pay homage at the grave of Christ—for the simple fact that **the tomb is empty**. A dead Savior is no good! For those who accept, and act upon, the evidence for Christ's deity provided by the resurrection, life is meaningful, rich, and full (see Paul's discussion in 1 Corinthians 15). For those who reject the resurrection, the vacant tomb will stand forever as eternity's greatest mystery, and one day will serve as their silent judge.

Conclusion

Who is Jesus of Nazareth? He had no formal rabbinical training (John 7:15). He possessed no material wealth (Luke 9:58; 2 Corinthians 8:9). Yet, through His teachings, He turned the world upside down (Acts 17:6). Clearly, as the evidence documents, He was, and is, both the Son of Man and the Son of God. He lived, and died, to redeem fallen mankind. He gave Himself a ransom (Matthew 20:28). He is God, Who predates, and will outlast, time itself (Philippians 2:5-11).

4

GOD'S PLAN FOR
MAN'S SALVATION

"And Jehovah God formed man of the dust of
the ground, and breathed into his nostrils the
breath of life; and man became a living soul"
(Genesis 2:7).

Of all the living beings that dwell on planet Earth, one solitary
creature was made "in the image of God." On day six of His creative
activity, God said: "Let us make man in our image, after our likeness.
And God created man in his own image, in the image of God created
he him; male and female created he them" (Genesis 1:26-27).

Mankind was not created in the physical image of God, of course,
because God, as a Spirit Being, has no physical image (John 4:24;
Luke 24:39; Matthew 16:17). Rather, mankind was fashioned in the
spiritual, rational, emotional, and volitional image of God (Ephesians
4:24; John 5:39-40; 7:17; Joshua 24:15; Isaiah 7:15). Humans are
superior to all other creatures. No other living being was given the facul-
ties, the capacities, the capabilities, the potential, or the dignity that God
instilled in each man and woman. Indeed, humankind is the peak,
the apex, the pinnacle of God's creation.

In its lofty position as the zenith of God's creative genius, mankind was endowed with certain responsibilities. Men and women were to be the stewards of the entire Earth (Genesis 1:28). They were to glorify God in their daily existence (Isaiah 43:7). And, they were to consider it their "whole duty" to serve the Creator faithfully throughout their brief sojourn on the Earth (Ecclesiastes 12:13).

Man's Predicament: Disobedience and Death

Unfortunately, the first man and woman used their volitional powers—and the free moral agency based on those powers—to rebel against their Maker. Finite man made some horribly evil choices, and so entered the spiritual state biblically designated as "sin." The Old Testament not only presents in vivid fashion the entrance of sin into the world through Adam and Eve (Genesis 3), but also alludes to the ubiquity of sin within the human race when it says: "There is no man that sinneth not" (1 Kings 8:46). Throughout its thirty-nine books, the Old Covenant discusses time and again both sin's presence amidst humanity and its destructive consequences. The great prophet Isaiah reminded God's people: "Behold, Jehovah's hand is not shortened that it cannot save; neither his ear heavy that it cannot hear: but your iniquities have separated between you and your God, and your sins have hid his face from you, so that he will not hear" (59:1-2).

The New Testament is no less clear in its assessment. The apostle John wrote: "Every one that doeth sin doeth also lawlessness; and sin is lawlessness" (1 John 3:4). Thus, sin is defined as the act of transgressing God's law. In fact, Paul observed that "where there is no law, neither is there transgression" (Romans 4:15). Had there been no law, there would have been no sin. But God **had** instituted divine law. And mankind freely chose to transgress that law. Paul reaffirmed the Old Testament concept of the universality of sin (1 Kings 8:46) when he stated that "all have sinned, and fall short of the glory of God" (Romans 3:23).

As a result, mankind's predicament became serious indeed. Ezekiel lamented: "The soul that sinneth, it shall die" (18:20a). Once again, the New Testament writers reaffirmed such a concept. Paul wrote: "Therefore, as through one man sin entered into the world, and death through sin; and so death passed unto all men, for that all sinned" (Romans 5:12). He then added that "the wages of sin is death" (Romans 6:23). Years later, James would write: "But each man is tempted, when he is drawn away by his own lust, and enticed. Then the lust, when it hath conceived, beareth sin: and the sin, when it is full-grown, bringeth forth death" (1:15-16).

As a result of mankind's sin, God placed the curse of death on the human race. While all men and women must die physically as a result of Adam and Eve's sin, each person dies spiritually for his or her own sins. Each person is responsible for himself, spiritually speaking. The theological position which states that we inherit the guilt of Adam's sin is false. We do not inherit the **guilt**; we inherit the **consequences**. And there is a great difference between the two.

Consider, as an illustration of this point, the family in which a drunken father arrives home late one evening, and in an alcoholic stupor severely beats his wife and children. His spouse and offspring suffer the consequences of his drunkenness, to be sure. But it would be absurd to suggest that they are guilty of it! The same concept applies in the spiritual realm. People die **physically** because of Adam's sin, but they die **spiritually** because of their own personal transgression of God's law. In Ezekiel 18:20, quoted earlier, the prophet went on to say: "The son shall not bear the iniquity of the father, neither shall the father bear the iniquity of the son: the righteousness of the righteous shall be upon him, and the wickedness of the wicked shall be upon him."

The Reality of Sin

The reality of sin is all around us, is it not? Consider the ways in which mankind has been affected by sin.

Physically—Disease and death were introduced into this world as a direct consequence of man's sin (Genesis 2:17; Romans 5:12).

Geophysically—Many features of the Earth's surface that allow for such tragedies as earthquakes, tornadoes, hurricanes, violent thunderstorms, etc. can be traced directly to the Great Flood of Noah's day (which came as the result of man's sin, Genesis 6:5ff.).

Culturally—The numerous communication problems that man experiences, due to the multiplicity of human languages, are traceable to ambitious rebellion on the part of our ancestors (Genesis 11:1-9).

Psychologically—Man generally is without the peace of mind for which his heart longs (look at the number of psychiatrists in the Yellow Pages of any telephone book!). Isaiah opined: "They have made them crooked paths; whosoever goeth therein doth not know peace" (59:8; cf. 57:21).

Spiritually—By sinning, man created a chasm between himself and God (Isaiah 59:2). Unless remedied, this condition will result in man's being unable to escape the "judgment of hell" (Matthew 23:33), and in his being separated from God throughout all eternity (Revelation 21:8; 22:18-19).

The key phrase in the discussion above is that man's sin will result in an eternal separation from God **unless remedied**. The question then becomes: Has God provided such a remedy? Thankfully, the answer is: Yes, He has.

God's Remedy for Sin

Regardless of how desperate, or how pitiful, man's condition has become, one thing is certain: God had no **obligation** to provide a means of salvation for the ungrateful creature who so haughtily turned away from Him, His law, and His beneficence. The Scriptures make this apparent when they discuss the fact that angels sinned (2 Peter 2:4; Jude 6), and yet "not to angels doth he give help, but he giveth help to the seed of Abraham" (Hebrews 2:16). The rebellious creatures that once inhabited the heavenly portals were not provided a redemptive plan. But man was! Little wonder the psalmist inquired: "What is **man**, that thou art mindful of **him**?" (Psalm 8:4, emp. added).

Why would God go to such great lengths for mankind, when His mercy was not even extended to the angels that once surrounded His throne? Whatever answers may be proffered, there can be little doubt that the Creator's efforts on behalf of sinful man are the direct result of pure love. As a loving God (1 John 4:8), He acted out of a genuine concern, not for His own desires, but instead for those of His creation. And let us be forthright in acknowledging that Jehovah's love for mankind was completely **undeserved**. The Scriptures make it clear that God decided to offer salvation—our "way home"—even though we were ungodly, sinners, and enemies (note the specific use of those terms in Romans 5:6-10). The apostle John rejoiced in the fact that: "Herein is love, not that we loved God, but that He loved us" (1 John 4:10).

God's love is universal, and thus not discriminatory in any fashion (John 3:16). He would have **all men** to be saved (1 Timothy 2:4)—**if they would be** (John 5:40)—for He is not willing that **any** should perish (2 Peter 3:9). And, Deity's love is unquenchable. Read Romans 8:35-39 and be thrilled! Only man's wanton rejection of God's love can put him beyond the practical appropriation of heaven's offer of mercy and grace.

God's Plan In Preparation

Did God understand that man would rebel, and stand in eventual need of salvation from the perilous state of his own sinful condition? The Scriptures make it clear that He did. Inspiration speaks of a divine plan set in place even "before the foundation of the world" (Ephesians 1:4; 1 Peter 1:20). After the initial fall of man, humankind dredged itself deeper and deeper into wickedness. When approximately a century of preaching by the righteous Noah failed to bring mankind back to God, Jehovah sent a worldwide flood to purge the Earth (Genesis 6-8). From the faithful Noah, several generations later, the renowned Abraham was descended, and, through him, eventually the Hebrew nation would be established. From that nation, the Messiah—God incarnate—would come.

Some four centuries following Abraham, the Lord, through His servant Moses, gave to the Hebrews the written revelation that came to be known as the Law of Moses. Basically, this law-system had three distinct purposes. First, its intent was to define sin and sharpen Israel's awareness of it. To use Paul's expression in the New Testament, the Law made "sin exceeding sinful" (Romans 7:7,13). Second, the law was designed to show man that he could not, by his own merit or efforts, save himself. For example, the Law demanded perfect obedience, and since no mere man could keep it perfectly, all stood condemned (Galatians 3:10-11). Thus, the Law underscored the need for a **Savior**—Someone Who could do for us what we were unable to do for ourselves. Third, in harmony with that need, the Old Testament pointed the way toward the coming of the Messiah. He was to be Immanuel—"God with us" (Matthew 1:23).

Mankind was prepared for the coming of the Messiah in several ways. **Theophanies** were temporary appearances of God in various forms (see Genesis 16:7ff.; 18:1ff.; 22:11ff., et al.). A careful examination of the facts leads to the conclusion that many of these manifestations were of the preincarnate Christ. In addition, the Old Testament contains **types** (pictorial previews) of the coming Messiah. For example, every bloody sacrifice was a symbol of the "Lamb of God that taketh away the sin of the world" (John 1:29). Finally, there are more than 300 **prophecies** containing countless minute details that speak of the coming Prince of Peace. These prophecies name the city in which He was to be born, the purpose of His earthly sojourn, and even the exact manner of His death.

The simple fact is, Jehovah left no stone unturned in preparing the world for the coming of the One Who would save mankind. Through a variety of avenues, He alerted Earth's inhabitants to the importance of Him Who was yet to come, and to the urgency of complete belief in Him.

God's Plan In Action

One of God's attributes, as expressed within Scripture, is that He is an absolutely **holy** Being (see Revelation 4:8; Isaiah 6:3). As such, He cannot, and will not, ignore the fact of sin. The prophet Habakkuk wrote: "Thou that art of purer eyes than to behold evil, and thou canst not look on perverseness" (1:13). Yet another of God's attributes is that He is absolutely **just**. Righteousness and justice are the very foundation of His throne (Psalm 89:14). The irresistible truth arising from the fact that God is both holy and just is **that sin must be punished!**

If God were a cold, vengeful Creator (as some infidels wrongly assert), He simply could have banished mankind from His divine presence forever and that would have been the end of the matter. But the truth is, He is not that kind of God! Our Creator is loving (1 John 4:8), and "rich in mercy" (Ephesians 2:4). Thus, the problem became: How could a loving, merciful God pardon rebellious humanity?

Paul addressed this very matter in Romans 3. How could God be just, and yet a justifier of sinful man? The answer: He would find someone to stand in for us—someone to receive His retribution, and to bear our punishment. That "someone" would be Jesus Christ, the Son of God. He would become a substitutionary sacrifice, and personally would pay the price for human salvation. In one of the most moving tributes ever written to the Son of God, Isaiah summarized the situation like this:

> But he was wounded for our transgressions, he was bruised for our iniquities; the chastisement of our peace was upon him; and with his stripes we are healed. All we like sheep have gone astray; we have turned every one to his own way; and Jehovah hath laid on Him the iniquity of us all (53:5-6).

Jehovah's intent was to extend grace and mercy freely—through the redemptive life and death of His Son (Romans 3:24ff.). As a member of the Godhead, Christ took upon Himself the form of a man. He came to Earth as a human being (John 1:1-4,14; Philippians 2:5-11; 1 Timothy 3:16), and thus shared our full nature and life-experiences. He even was tempted in all points, just we are, yet He never yielded to that temptation (Hebrews 4:15).

But what has this to do with us? Since Christ was tried (Isaiah 28:16), and yet found perfect (2 Corinthians 5:21; 1 Peter 2:22), He alone could satisfy heaven's requirement for justice. He alone could serve as the "propitiation" (atoning sacrifice) for our sins. Just as the lamb without blemish that was used in Old Testament sacrifices could be the (temporary) propitiation for the Israelites' sins, so the "Lamb of God" (John 1:29) could be the (permanent) propitiation for mankind's sins.

In the gift of Christ, Heaven's mercy was extended; in the death of the Lamb of God, divine justice was satisfied; and, in the resurrection of Christ, God's plan was documented and sealed historically forever!

Mankind's Appropriation of God's Gift of Salvation

As wonderful as God's gift of salvation is, there is one thing it is not. It is not **unconditional**. Mankind has a part to play in this process. While the gift of salvation itself is free (in the sense that the price levied already has been paid by Christ), God will not **force** salvation on anyone. Rather, man must—by the exercise of his personal volition and free moral agency—do something to accept the pardon that heaven offers. What is that "something"?

In His manifold dealings with mankind, Jehovah has stressed repeatedly the principle that man, if he would be justified, must live "by faith" (see Habakkuk 2:4; Romans 1:17; Galatians 3:11; Hebrews 10:38). Salvation has been available across the centuries, conditioned upon God's foreknowledge of the atoning death of Christ upon the Cross at Calvary (see Galatians 4:4-5; Hebrews 9:15-17; 10:1ff.). Yet "living by faith" never denoted a mere "mental ascent" of certain facts. Instead, "living by faith" denoted **active obedience**.

Faith consists of three elements: (1) an acknowledgment of historical facts; (2) a willingness to trust the Lord; and (3) a wholehearted submission (obedience) to the divine will. Further, it should be remembered that faith has not always—for all men, in all circumstances—required the same things. It always has required obedience, but obedience itself has not always demanded the same response.

For example, in God's earliest dealings with men, obedient faith required that those men offer animal sacrifices at the family altar (Genesis 4:4). Later, God dealt with the nation of Israel, giving them the Law at Mount Sinai (Exodus 20). Under that Law, animal sacrifices continued, along with the observance of certain feast days and festivals. Acceptable faith, under whatever law that was then in force, demanded obedience to the will of God.

The Scriptures are clear that "obedience of faith" (Romans 1:5; 16:26) is based on the Word of God (Romans 10:13), and that both the faith and the obedience are demonstrated by **action**. Hebrews 11, in fact, devotes itself to an examination of that very concept. "By faith" Abel **offered**. "By faith" Noah **prepared**. "By faith" Abraham **obeyed**. "By faith," Moses **refused**. And so on. Even the casual reader cannot help but be impressed with the heroes of faith listed in Hebrews 11:32-40, and the **action** they took **because of their faith**. Writing by inspiration, James observed that faith, divorced from obedience, is dead (James 2:26). What, then, is involved in this "obedience of faith" in regard to salvation? What must a person **do** to be saved?

Several critically important questions need to be asked here. First, where is salvation found? Paul told Timothy: "Therefore I endure all things for the elect's sake, that they also may obtain **the salvation which is in Christ Jesus** with eternal glory" (2 Timothy 2:10, emp. added).

Second, where are all spiritual blessings found? They are found only "in Christ." Paul wrote in Ephesians 1:3: "Blessed be the God and Father of our Lord Jesus Christ, who hath blessed us with every spiritual blessing in the heavenly places **in Christ**" (emp. added).

Third, and most importantly, how, then, does one get "into Christ"? In other words, how does the alien sinner rid himself of his soul-damning sin? What "obedience of faith" is required to appropriate the free gift of salvation that places him "in Christ"?

The Road Home: Salvation Through "Obedience of Faith"

The only way to find the "road home" to heaven is to follow God's directions **exactly**. There are numerous things God has commanded that a person **do** in order to enjoin the "obedience of faith" and thereby receive the free gift of salvation. According to God's Word, in order to be saved a person must do the following.

First, the sinner must **hear** God's Word (Romans 10:17). Obviously, one cannot follow God's commands if he has not heard them, so God commanded that people hear what He has said regarding salvation.

Second, one who is lost cannot be saved if he does not **believe** what he hears. So, God commanded that belief ensue (John 3:16; Acts 16:31).

Third, one who is lost cannot obtain salvation if he is unwilling to **repent** of his sins and seek forgiveness (Luke 13:3). Without repentance he will continue in sin; thus, God commanded repentance.

Fourth, since Christ is the basis of our salvation, God commanded the penitent sinner to **confess** Him before men as the Son of God (Romans 10:9-10).

However, this is not all that God commanded. Hearing, believing, repentance, and confession will not rid one of his sin. The overriding question is: **How does one get rid of sin**? Numerous times within the pages of the New Testament, that question is asked and answered. The Jews who had murdered Christ, and to whom Peter spoke on the Day of Pentecost when he ushered in the Christian age, asked that question. Peter's sermon had convicted them. They were convinced that they were sinners and, as such, desperately in need of salvation at the hand of an almighty God. Their question then became: "Brethren, what shall we do?" (Acts 2:37). Peter's response could not have been any clearer. He told them: "Repent ye, and **be baptized** every one of you in the name of Jesus Christ **unto the remission of your sins**" (Acts 2:38). Saul, who later would become Paul, the famous apostle to the Gentiles, needed an answer to that same question. While on a trip to Damascus for the explicit purpose of persecuting Christians, Saul was blinded (see Acts 22). Realizing his plight, he asked: "What shall I do, Lord?" (Acts 22:10). When God's servant, Ananias, appeared to Saul in the city, he answered Saul's question by commanding: "And now why tarriest thou? Arise, and **be baptized, and wash away thy sins**" (Acts 22:16).

What, then, is the correct biblical answer regarding how one rids himself of soul-damning sin? The biblical solution is that the person who has heard the gospel, who has believed its message, who has repented of past sins, and who has confessed Christ as Lord must then—in order to receive remission (forgiveness) of sins—be baptized. [The English word "baptize" is a transliteration of the Greek word *baptizo,* meaning to immerse, dip, plunge beneath, or submerge (Thayer, 1958, p. 94).]

Further, it is baptism that puts a person "in Christ." Paul told the first-century Christians in Rome:

> Or are ye ignorant that all we who were baptized into Christ Jesus were baptized into his death? We were buried therefore with him through baptism into death: that like as Christ was raised from the dead through the glory of the Father, so we also might walk in newness of life (Romans 6:3-4).

Paul told the Galatians: "For as many of you as were **baptized into Christ** did put on Christ" (3:37, emp. added). Little wonder, then, that Peter spoke of baptism as that which saves (1 Peter 3:21).

Numerous New Testament writers made the point that it is only when we come into contact with Christ's blood that our sins can be washed away (Ephesians 1:7-8; Revelation 5:9; Romans 5:8-9; Hebrews 9:12-14). The question arises: **When** did Jesus shed His blood? The answer, of course, is that He shed His blood on the Cross at His death (John 19:31-34). Where, and how, does one come into contact with Christ's blood to obtain the forgiveness of sin that such contact ensures? Paul answered that question when he wrote to the Christians in Rome. It is only in baptism that contact with the blood, and the death, of Christ is made (Romans 6:3-11). Further, the ultimate hope of our resurrection (to live with Him in heaven) is linked to baptism. Paul wrote of "having been buried with him in baptism, wherein ye were raised with him through faith in the working of God, who raised him from the dead" (Colossians 2:12). If we are not baptized, we remain in sin. If we are not baptized, we have no hope of the resurrection that leads to heaven.

Baptism, of course, is no less, or more, important than any other of God's commands regarding what to do to be saved (see Jackson, 1997c). But it is **essential**, and one cannot be saved without it. Is baptism a command of God? Yes (Acts 10:48). Is baptism where the remission of sins occurs? Yes (Acts 2:38; Acts 22:16; 1 Peter 3:21).

Some, who no doubt mean well, teach that a person is saved by "faith only." That is, people are taught simply to "pray and ask Jesus to come into their hearts" so that they might be saved from their sins. This teaching, though widespread, is completely at odds with the Bible's specific instructions regarding what one must do to be saved.

First, the Scriptures teach clearly that God does not hear (i.e., hear to respond with forgiveness) the prayer of an alien sinner (Psalm 34:15-16; Proverbs 15:29; Proverbs 28:9). Thus, the sinner can pray as long and as hard as he wants, but God has stated plainly how a person is to be saved. This makes perfect sense, since in John 14:6 Christ taught: "I am the way, and the truth, and the life; no one cometh to the Father but by me." The alien sinner cannot approach God on his own, and, as an alien sinner, has no advocate to do so on his behalf. That is one of the spiritual blessings reserved for Christians (Ephesians 1:3). Thus, it is fruitless for an alien sinner to pray to God to "send Jesus into his heart." God does not hear (i.e., hear to respond to) such a request.

Second, the Scriptures plainly teach that man **cannot be saved by faith alone**. James, in his epistle, remarked that indeed, a man may be justified (i.e., saved), but "not only by faith" (James 2:24). This, too, makes perfectly good sense. As James had observed only a few verses earlier: "Thou believest that God is one; thou doest well; the demons also believe, and shudder" (James 2:19). It is not enough merely to believe. Even the demons who inhabit the eternal regions of hell believe. But they hardly are saved (see 2 Peter 2:4). It is obvious, therefore, that mere faith **alone** is insufficient to save mankind.

Also, where, exactly, in the Scriptures does it teach that, in order to be saved, one should to "pray to ask Jesus to come into his heart"? Through the years, I have asked many within various religious groups this important question. But I have yet to find anyone who could provide a single biblical reference to substantiate such a claim.

Salvation is not conditioned on prayer; it is conditioned on the "obedience of faith." The case of Saul provides a good example. As Christ's enemy-turned-penitent, he prayed earnestly while living in his blind state in the city of Damascus. Yet the fact remains that his sins were removed ("washed away") only when he obeyed God's command (as verbalized by Ananias) to be baptized. Prayer could not wash away Saul's sins. But the Lord's blood could—at the point of baptism (Hebrews 9:22; Ephesians 5:26).

Objections to God's Plan of Salvation

When the topic of salvation is discussed, it is not unusual to hear certain objections to God's designated plan. At times, such objections result from a misunderstanding of the steps involved in the salvation process (or the reasons for those steps). On occasion, however, the objections result from a stubborn refusal to acquiesce to God's commands regarding what constitutes salvation. I would like to consider three such objections here.

Is Salvation the Result of "Baptismal Regeneration"?

Is the forgiveness of sins that results from being baptized due to some special power within the water? No. "Baptismal regeneration" is the idea that there is a miraculous power in the water that produces salvation (i.e., regeneration). As Wayne Jackson has noted: "..the notion that baptism is a 'sacrament' which has a sort of mysterious, innate power to remove the contamination of sin—independent of personal faith and a volitional submission to God's plan of redemption" —is plainly at odds with biblical teaching (1997b, 32:45). An examination of the Old Testament (which serves as our "tutor" [Galatians 3: 24] and contains things "for our learning" [Romans 15:4]) provides important instruction regarding this principle. When Naaman the leper was told by Elijah to dip seven times in the Jordan River, at first he refused, but eventually obeyed—and was healed. However, there was no meritorious power in the muddy waters of the Jordan. Naaman was healed because He did exactly what God commanded him to do, in exactly the way God commanded him to do it.

This was true of the Israelites' salvation as well. On one occasion when they sinned, and God began to slay them for their unrighteousness, those who wished to repent and be spared were commanded to look upon a brass serpent on a pole in the midst of the camp (Numbers 21:1-9). There was no meritorious power in the serpent. Rather, the Israelites were saved from destruction because they did exactly what God commanded them to do, in exactly the way God commanded them to do it.

The New Testament presents the same principle. Jesus once encountered a man born blind (John 9). Then Lord spat on the ground, made a spittle/clay potion, and placed it over the man's eyes. He then instructed the man to "go, wash in the pool of Siloam" (John 9: 7). Was there medicinal power in Siloam's waters? No. It was the man's obedient faith that produced the end-result, not some miraculous power in the water.

What would have happened if the man had refused to obey Christ, or had altered the Lord's command? Suppose the man had reasoned: "If I wash in Siloam, some may think I am trusting in the **water** to be healed. Others may think that I am attempting to perform some kind of 'work' to 'merit' regaining my sight. Therefore I simply will 'have faith in' Christ, but I will **not** dip in the pool of Siloam." Would the man have been healed? Most certainly not!

What if Noah, during the construction of the ark, had followed God's instructions to the letter, except for the fact that he decided to build the ark out of a material other than the gopher wood that God had commanded? Would Noah and his family have been saved? Most certainly not! Noah would have been guilty of violating God's commandments, since he had not done **exactly** as God commanded him. Did not Jesus Himself say: "If ye love me, ye will **keep My commandments**" (John 14:15, emp. added)?

Peter used the case of Noah to discuss the relationship of baptism to salvation. He stated unequivocally that baptism is involved in salvation when he noted that, just as Noah and his family were transported from a polluted environment of corruption into a realm of deliverance, so in baptism we are moved from the polluted environment of defilement into a realm of redemption. It is by baptism that one enters "into Christ" (Romans 6:4; Galatians 3:27), wherein salvation is found (2 Timothy 2:10). In Ephesians 5:26 and Titus 3:35, Paul described baptism as a "washing of water" or a "washing of regeneration" wherein the sinner is "cleansed" or "saved." [Baptist theologian A.T. Robertson admitted that both of these passages refer specifically to water baptism (1931, 4:607).] The power of baptism to remove sin lies not in the water, but in the God Who commanded the sinner to be baptized in the first place.

Is Baptism a Human Work?

Is baptism a meritorious human work? No. But is it required for a person to be saved? Yes. How is this possible? The Bible clearly teaches that we are **not** saved by works (Titus 3:4-7; Ephesians 2:9).

Yet the Bible clearly teaches we **are** saved by works (James 2:14-24). Since inspiration guarantees that the Scriptures never will contradict themselves, it is obvious that **two different kinds of works** are under consideration in these passages.

The New Testament mentions at least four kinds of works: (1) works of the Law of Moses (Galatians 2:16; Romans 3:20); (2) works of the flesh (Galatians 5:19-21); (3) works of merit (Titus 3:4-7); and (4) works resulting from obedience of faith (James 2:14-24). This last category often is referred to as "works of God." This phrase does not mean works **performed by** God; rather, the intent is "works **required and approved by** God" (Thayer, 1958, p. 248; cf. Jackson, 1997c, 32:47). Consider the following example from Jesus' statements in John 6:27-29:

> Work not for the food which perisheth, but for the food which abideth unto eternal life.... They said therefore unto him, What must we do, that we may work the **works of God**? Jesus answered and said unto them, This is the **work of God**, that ye believe on him whom he hath sent.

Within this context, Christ made it clear that there are works which humans must do to receive eternal life. Moreover, the passage affirms that believing itself is a work ("This is the **work** of God, that ye **believe** on him whom he hath sent"). It therefore follows that if one is saved **without any type of works**, then he is saved **without faith**, because **faith is a work**. Such a conclusion would throw the Bible into hopeless confusion!

In addition, it should be noted that repentance from sin is a divinely appointed work for man to perform prior to his reception of salvation. The people of ancient Nineveh "repented" at Jonah's preaching (Matthew 12:41), yet the Old Testament record relates that "God saw their **works**, that they turned from their evil way" (Jonah 3:10). Thus, if one can be saved without **any kind** of works, he can be saved **without repentance**. Yet Jesus Himself declared that without repentance, one will surely perish (Luke 13:3,5).

But what about baptism? The New Testament **specifically excludes** baptism from the class of human meritorious works unrelated to redemption. The context of Titus 3:4-7 reveals the following information. (1) We **are not saved** by works of righteousness that we do by ourselves (i.e., according to any plan or course of action that we devised—see Thayer, p. 526). (2) We **are saved** by the "washing of regeneration" (i.e., baptism), exactly as 1 Peter 3:21 states. (3) Thus, baptism is excluded from all works of human righteousness that men contrive, but is itself a "work of God" (i.e., required and approved by God) necessary for salvation. When one is raised from the watery grave of baptism, it is according to the "working of God" (Colossians 2:12), and not any man-made plan. No one can suggest (justifiably) that baptism is a meritorious work of human design. When we are baptized, we are completely passive, and thus hardly can have performed any kind of "work." Instead, we have obeyed God through saving faith. Our "works of God" were belief, repentance, confession, and baptism—all commanded by the Scriptures of one who would receive salvation as the free gift of God (Romans 6:23).

Is the Baptism Associated with Salvation Holy Spirit Baptism?

To circumvent the connection between water baptism and salvation, some have suggested that the baptism discussed in passages such as Acts 2:38, Acts 22:16, and 1 Peter 3:21 is Holy Spirit baptism. But such a position cannot be correct. Christ commanded His followers—after His death and ascension—to go into all the world and "make disciples of all the nations, baptizing them into the name of the Father and of the Son and of the Holy Spirit" (Matthew 28:18-20). That same command applies no less to Christians today.

During the early parts of the first century, we know there was more than one baptism in existence (e.g., John's baptism, Holy Spirit baptism, Christ's baptism, etc.). But by the time Paul wrote his epistle to the Christians who lived in Ephesus, **only one** of those baptisms remained. He stated specifically in Ephesians 4:4-5: "There is one body, and one Spirit, even as also ye were called in one hope of your calling; one Lord, one faith, **one baptism**." Which **one** baptism remained? One thing we know for certain: Christ never would give His disciples a command that they could not carry out.

The Scriptures, however, teach that Jesus administers baptism of the Holy Spirit (Matthew 3:11; Luke 3:15-17). Yet Christians were commanded to baptize those whom they taught, and who believed (John 3:16), repented of their sins (Luke 13:3), and confessed Christ as the Son of God (Matthew 10:32). It is clear, then, that the baptism commanded by Christ was not Holy Spirit baptism. If it were, Christ would be put in the untenable position of having commanded His disciples to do something they could not do—baptize in the Holy Spirit. However, they **could** baptize in **water**, which is exactly what they did. And that is exactly what we still are doing today. Baptism in the Holy Spirit no longer is available; only water baptism remains, and is the one true baptism commanded by Christ for salvation (Ephesians 4:4-5; Mark 16:16; Acts 2:38).

When a person does precisely what the Lord has commanded, he has not "merited" or "earned" salvation. Rather, his obedience is evidence of his faith (James 2:18). Are we saved by God's grace? Indeed we are (Ephesians 2:8-9). But the fact that we are saved by grace does not negate human responsibility in obeying God's commands. Every person who wishes to be saved must exhibit the "obedience of faith" commanded within God's Word (Romans 1:5; 16:26). A part of that obedience is adhering to God's command to be baptized.

Conclusion

The biblical message—from Genesis 1 to Revelation 22—is that mankind is in a woefully sinful condition, and desperately in need of help in order to find his way "back home." A corollary to that message is that God takes no pleasure in the death of the wicked (Ezekiel 18:23; 33:11), and genuinely desires that all should be saved (John 3:

16). But in order to be saved, one must do **exactly** what God commanded, in **exactly** the way God commanded it. When a person hears, believes, repents, confesses, and is baptized for the forgiveness of his sins, that person becomes a Christian—nothing more, and nothing less. God Himself then adds that Christian to His Son's one true body—the church. The child of God who remains faithful even unto death (Revelation 2:10) is promised a crown of life and eternity in heaven as a result of his faith, his obedience, God's mercy, and God's grace (John 14:15; Ephesians 2:8-9; Romans 1:5). What a joyous thought —to live the "abundant life" (John 10:10b) with a "peace that passeth understanding" (Philippians 4:7) here and now, and then to be rewarded with a home in heaven in the hereafter (John 14:2-3). What a joyous thought indeed!

[AUTHOR'S NOTE: I would like to thank my friend and colleague, Wayne Jackson, for allowing me to employ in this article material on God's plan of salvation from the *Study Course in Christian Evidences* that he and I co-authored (see Thompson and Jackson, 1992).]

5

THE ESSENTIALITY
AND SINGULARITY
OF CHRIST'S CHURCH

But when the fulness of the time came," the apostle Paul wrote, "God sent forth his Son, born of a woman, born under the law, that he might redeem them that were under the law, that we might receive the adoption of sons" (Galatians 4:4-5). God incarnate had come to Earth, bringing the "good news" about the last and final covenant that Heaven would make with man. The series of events that began with the birth of Christ in Bethlehem, and culminated in His death, burial, and resurrection outside Jerusalem approximately thirty-three years later, stirred a whirlwind of controversy in the first century. Nineteen centuries later, it still does.

To the Christian, there is little of more importance than the proclamation and defense of the Old Jerusalem Gospel that is able to save men's souls. Christianity did not come into the world with a whimper, but a bang. It was not in the first century, neither is it intended to be in the twentieth, something "done in a corner." Instead, it arrived like a trumpet's clarion call.

Christ spent three-and-a-half years teaching in order to make disciples. When finally He was ready to call them to action, it was not for a quiet retreat into the peaceful, nearby hills. He never intended that they be "holy men" who set themselves apart to spend each hour of every day in serene meditation. Rather, they were to be soldiers—fit for a spiritual battle against forces of evil (Ephesians 6:10-17). Jesus called for action, self-denial, uncompromising love for truth, and zeal coupled with knowledge. His words to those who would follow Him were: "If any man would come after me, let him deny himself, and take up his cross, and follow me" (Mark 8:34). And many did.

The teaching did not stop when Christ left to return to His home in heaven. He had trained others—apostles and disciples—to continue the task He had begun. They were sent to the uttermost parts of the world with the mandate to proclaim the gospel boldly through preaching and teaching (Matthew 28:18-20). This they did daily (Acts 5:42). The result was additional, new disciples. They too, then, were instructed and grounded in the fundamentals of God's Word (Acts 2:42) and sent on their way to teach still others.

The results were extraordinary indeed. In a single day, in a single city, over 3,000 constituted the original church as a result of the teaching they had heard from Christ's apostles (see Acts 2:41). In fact, so effective was this kind of instruction that the enemies of Christianity attempted to prohibit any further public teaching (Acts 4:18; 5:28), yet to no avail. Nineteen centuries later, the theme of the Cross still is alive, vibrant, and forceful. Christianity's central message, the manner in which that message was taught, and the dedication of those into whose hands it had been placed, were too powerful for even its bitterest foes to abate or defeat. That Christianity continues to be taught, and to thrive, is evidence aplenty of this fact.

While it may be true to say that some religions flourish best in secrecy, such is not the case with Christianity. It is intended both to be presented, and to be defended, in the marketplace of ideas. In addition, while some religions eschew open investigation and critical evaluation, Christianity welcomes both. Of all the major religions based upon an individual rather than a mere ideology, it is the only one that claims, and can document, an empty tomb for its Founder. Furthermore, Christians, unlike adherents to some other religions, do not have an option regarding the distribution and/or dissemination of their faith. The efficacy of God's saving grace—as made possible through His Son, Jesus Christ—is a message that all accountable people need to hear, and one that Christians are commanded to proclaim (John 3:16; Matthew 28:18-20; cf. Ezekiel 33:7-9).

Christ's Church—His Singular, Unique Body of Saved Believers

At Caesarea Philippi, situated at the base of Mount Hermon that rises over seven thousand feet above it, Jesus asked His disciples how the public viewed Him. "Who do men say that the Son of man is?," He inquired (Matthew 16:13). The reply of the disciples was: "Some say, John the Baptist; some, Elijah; and others, Jeremiah, or one of the prophets" (16:14). But Jesus delved deeper when He asked the disciples: "But who say ye that I am?" (16:15). Ever the impulsive one, Simon Peter quickly answered: "Thou art the Christ, the Son of the living God" (16:16). Jesus' response to Peter was this:

> Blessed art thou, Simon Bar-Jonah: for flesh and blood hath not revealed it unto thee, but my Father who is in heaven. And I also say unto thee, that thou art Peter, and upon this rock I will build my church; and the gates of Hades shall not prevail against it (16:17-18).

Jesus had come "in the fulness of time" to bring the one thing that all the Earth's inhabitants needed. From Cain, the first murderer, to the lawless men who eventually would put Him to death on the cross, mankind desperately needed the salvation that the heavenly plan would provide. In writing to the young evangelist Timothy, Paul observed that it had been God's plan to save men through Christ even before the foundation of the world. He wrote of God, "who saved us, and called us with a holy calling, not according to our works, but according to his own purpose and grace, which was given us in Christ Jesus before times eternal" (2 Timothy 1:9). Through His foreknowledge, God knew that man one day would need redemption from sin. In fact, throughout the history of Israel, God made both promises and prophecies concerning a coming kingdom and its King. The promise was that from David's seed, God would build a "house" and "kingdom" (2 Samuel 7:11-17—a promise, incidentally, that was reaffirmed in Psalm 132:11 and preached as reality by Peter in Acts 2:29-34 when the church began). Seven hundred years before Christ's arrival, the prophet Isaiah foretold:

> For unto us a child is born, unto us a son is given; and the government shall be upon his shoulder: and his name shall be called Wonderful, Counsellor, Mighty God, Everlasting Father, Prince of Peace. Of the increase of his government and of peace there shall be no end, upon the throne of David, and upon his kingdom, to establish it, and to uphold it with justice and with righteousness from henceforth even for ever. The zeal of Jehovah of hosts will perform this (Isaiah 9:6-7).

Thus, Christ's exclamation to Peter that the building of His church would be upon a "rock" was nothing more than what the Old Testament prophets had foretold hundreds of years before. Isaiah prophesied: "Therefore, thus saith the Lord Jehovah, Behold, I lay in Zion for a foundation a stone, a tried stone, a precious corner-stone of sure foundation: he that believeth shall not be in haste" (Isaiah 28:16). Later, Peter himself—through inspiration, and no doubt with the events of Caesarea Philippi still fresh on his mind—would make reference to this very rock foundation when he wrote about the "living stone, rejected indeed of men....The stone which the builders rejected, the same was made the head of the corner" (1 Peter 2:4,7). In fact, even Jesus Himself mentioned the "rejected stone" of Old Testament allusion. In Matthew 21:42, Mark 12:10, and Luke 20:17, He made reference to the psalmist's statement about "the stone which the builders rejected is become the head of the corner" (Psalm 118:22), and applied the rejection of the stone by the builders to the Sanhedrin's rejection and repudiation of Him.

Sadly, some today erroneously teach that Christ's church was established out of desperation as an "emergency measure" set in motion when the Jews rejected Him as Savior. The basis for such a view is the idea that Jesus presented Himself to the Jewish nation as its Messiah but was rebuffed—a rejection that came as an unexpected surprise to Him and His Father. Christ's failure to convince the Jews of His rightful place as their King forced Him to have to re-evaluate, and eventually delay, His plans—His intention being to re-establish His kingdom at some distant point in the future. In the meantime, the story goes, He established the church to allay temporarily the complete failure of His mission.

However, such a view ignores the inspired writers' observations that "before times eternal" God had set in motion His plan for man's salvation as His Son's church. [The Greek word *ekklesia*, translated "church" in the English, denotes God's "called out."] It ignores the Old Testament prophecies that specifically predicted Christ's rejection by the Jews. And, it ignores Christ's own allusions to those prophecies during His earthly ministry. But worst of all, it impeaches the omniscience of both God and His Son by suggesting that they were "caught off guard" by the Jews' rejection of Christ as the Messiah, thus causing Heaven's emissary to have to rethink His plans. What an offensive and unscriptural view this is!

Jesus **was** a man with a mission—and He completed successfully what He had come to accomplish. Deity had come to Earth, taking the form of a servant (Philippians 2:7) to communicate to man the truth (John 8:32) about the lost state in which man now found himself (Romans 3:23; 6:23), and to pay the ransom for man (Matthew 20:28), thereby extricating him from a situation from which he could not extricate himself (Jeremiah 10:23).

When Christ died upon the cross, it was not for any sin that He personally had committed. Though He was tempted in all points like as we are, He did not sin (Hebrews 4:15). When Peter wrote that Jesus "did not sin," he employed a verbal tense which suggests that the Lord never sinned—not even once (1 Peter 2:22). Isaiah repeatedly emphasized the substitutionary nature of the Lord's death when he wrote: "But he was wounded for our transgressions, he was bruised for our iniquities; the chastisement of our peace was upon him; and with his stripes we are healed.... Jehovah hath laid on him the iniquity of us all" (Isaiah 53:5-6). When the prophet declared that our "iniquity" was laid upon the Son of God, he employed a figure of speech known as metonymy (wherein one thing is used to designate another). In this case, the cause is being used for the effect. In other words, God did not actually put our **sins** upon Christ; He put the **penalty** of our wrongs upon His Son at Calvary. Yet, in spite of the fact that all sinners deserve to be lost, God provided a way to "escape the judgment of hell" (Matthew 23:33).

Jesus made it clear that He would provide this way of escape through a plan that would result in the establishment of His church—i.e., His body of "the called out." The first messianic prophecy was to be fulfilled: Satan would bruise the Lord's heel, but the Lord would overcome, and bruise Satan's head (Genesis 3:15). Against the building of Christ's church, not even the Gates of Hades could prevail (Matthew 16:18).

Further, there would be one and only one church. Paul wrote that Christ "is the head of **the body, the church**" (Colossians 1:18). In Ephesians 1:22, he stated concerning Christ that God "gave him to be head over all things to the church, **which is his body.**" Thus, Paul clearly identified the body as the church. Three chapters later, however, in Ephesians 4:4, Paul stated: "There is **one body.**" Expressed logically, one might reason as follows:

There is one body (Ephesians 4:4).
But Christ is the Savior of the body (Ephesians 5:22).
Thus, Christ is the Savior of **one body.**

And,

Christ is the Savior of one body.
But the body is the church (Ephesians 1:22-23; Colossians1:18,24).
Thus, Christ is the Savior of **one** church.

The body, Christ's church, would be known as "the church of the Lord" (Acts 20:28), "the church of God" (1 Corinthians 1:2; Galatians 1:13), "the house of God" (1 Timothy 3:15), "the household of faith" (Galatians 6:10), and "the kingdom of God" (Acts 28:23,31). The Lord's people were to bear Christ's name (Acts 11:26; 26:28; 1 Peter 4:16). The church would be His bride (Revelation 21:2), His wife (Revelation 19:7-8), and His kingdom (Revelation 1:9). Those in it would be victorious over Satan and death forever (1 Corinthians 15:26,54-56; 2 Timothy 1:9-10).

Unfortunately, men sought to alter the divine plan, and to infuse it with their own personal belief systems. Thus, the concept of denominationalism was born. Denominationalism, however, is unknown to, and unauthorized by, the Word of God. A denomination is defined as: "a class or kind having a specific name or value...." We speak of various monetary denominations—a five-dollar bill, a ten-dollar bill, etc. They all are different. The same is true of religious denominations. They all are different.

Denominationalism ignores the singularity and uniqueness of the true church, and establishes various groups teaching conflicting doctrines that are antagonistic both to the Bible and to each other. It also ignores the church's relationship to Christ, described so beautifully in Ephesians 5 where Paul reminded first-century Christians that "the husband is the head of the wife, as Christ also is the head of the church" (5:23). The apostle's point was this: In a physical context, the wife is the bride and the husband is the bridegroom; in a spiritual context, the church is the bride and Christ is the bridegroom (the same point reiterated by John in Revelation 21:9). In Acts, Peter discussed Christ's relationship to His church when he observed that "neither is there any other name under heaven, that is given among men, wherein we must be saved" (Acts 4:12).

Denominations are man-made institutions that neither are recognized in, nor sanctioned by, the Word of God. The simple truth of the matter is that John the Baptist—while a marvelous harbinger of the Messiah—did not die to establish the church. Why, then, be a member of a denomination bearing his name? As great a reformer as Martin Luther was, the fact remains that he did not die to establish the church. Why, then, be a member of a denomination bearing his name? The early church's presbyters (i.e., elders, bishops, overseers) did not give their lives on a cross to establish the church. Why, then, be a member of a denomination named after such men? The Bible—although it prophesies the coming of the church and documents its arrival—did not make possible the church. Why, then, be a member of a "Bible church"? Instead, should not Christians seek to be simply a member of the singular church that honors Christ's authority, and that He purchased with His blood? It is His bride; He is its bridegroom. His congregations are called the "churches of Christ" (Romans 16:16).

Those who are true New Testament Christians are those who have done exactly what God has commanded them to do to be saved, in exactly the way God has commanded that it be done. In so doing, they have not "joined" some man-made religious denomination that, like a five-dollar bill is one denomination among many others, is simply one religious group among many others. If the church is the body, and there is only one body, then there is only one church. Further, one does not "join" the church. The Scriptures teach that as a person is saved, God Himself "adds" that person to the one true church (Acts 2:41) that bears His Son's name.

Christ's Church—His Divinely Designed, Blood-Bought, Spirit-Filled Kingdom

During His earthly ministry, Jesus taught: "All authority hath been given unto me in heaven and on earth" (Matthew 28:18). Having such authority from His Father, He alone possessed the right to be Head of the church, His singular body of believers (Ephesians 1:22-23; Colossians 1:18). Recognizing Christ's position as authoritative Head of the church, Paul was constrained to remind Christians: "And whatsoever ye do, in word or in deed, do all in the name of [by the authority of—BT] the Lord Jesus" (Colossians 3:17).

Christ announced while on Earth that He would build His church (Matthew 16:18). It would be divinely designed (John 10:25; Acts 2:23), blood bought (Acts 20:28), and Spirit filled (1 Corinthians 6:19-20; Romans 8:9-10). On Pentecost following the Lord's death, burial, and resurrection, Peter rebuked the Jews for their duplicity in killing God's Son, and convicted them of their sin of murder (Acts 2:22-23). Luke recorded that they were "pricked in their heart" and sought to make restitution and be forgiven (Acts 2:27). On that fateful day, at least 3,000 people were added together by God to constitute Christ's church (Acts 2:41). Later, Luke noted that great fear fell upon the **whole church** as a result of God's having disciplined sinners within it (Acts 5:11). There is no doubt that the church was established in Christ's generation.

The Bible speaks of the church as Christ's kingdom. Jesus said the time for its coming had been "fulfilled" (Mark 1:15) and that the kingdom was as near as the generation of people to whom He spoke, since some of them would not taste of death before they saw the kingdom of heaven come (Mark 9:1). Paul taught that the church is constituted of saints (1 Corinthians 1:1-2). But when he wrote his epistle to the Colossians (c. A.D. 62), he specifically stated that by that time the saints in the church at Colossae were subjects in "the kingdom of the Son of his love" (Colossians 1:13).

If the kingdom had not been established, then Paul erred in saying that the Colossians already were in it. [Those who teach that the church and the kingdom are separate, and that the kingdom has yet to arrive, must contend that there are living on the Earth today some of the very people to whom Jesus spoke nearly 2,000 years ago—since He stated that some who heard Him **would not die until the kingdom had come** (Mark 9:1).]

The New Testament teaches that the **church** is composed of individuals purchased with the blood of Christ (Acts 20:28), and that those so purchased were made to be a **kingdom** (Revelation 1:5-6; 5:9-10). Since the church and the kingdom both are composed of blood-purchased individuals, the church and the kingdom must be the same. And since the Christians that constitute the church were themselves translated into the kingdom, it is conclusive that the church and the kingdom **are** the same. The establishment of the kingdom coincided with the establishment of the church. Not only did the Lord foretell both the establishment of the kingdom and the church in His generation, but the New Testament writers spoke of both the church and the kingdom as being in existence during the very generation of His arrival (i.e., the first century).

Christ's Triumphant Church

From the first to the last of His earthly ministry, Jesus admonished those who would be His disciples that they would be both controversial, and persecuted. He warned them:

> Think not that I came to send peace on the earth: I came not to send peace, but a sword. For I came to set a man at variance against his father and the daughter against her mother, and the daughter in law against her mother in law: and a man's foes shall be they of his own household (Matthew 10:34-36).

Jesus wanted no misunderstanding about the trials and tribulations His followers would endure. He constantly reminded them of such (Matthew 10:16,39; 16:24; 24:9; John 15:2,18,20; 16:1-2; 21:18-19). While He desired that men be at peace with men, His primary goal was to bring men to a peaceful, covenant relationship with God. In addressing the Christians at Rome, Paul wrote:

> Who shall separate us from the love of Christ? shall tribulation, or anguish, or persecution, or famine, or nakedness, or peril, or sword?... Nay, in all these things we are more than conquerors through him that loved us. For I am persuaded that neither death, nor life, nor angels, nor principalities, nor things present, nor things to come, nor powers, nor height, nor depth, nor any other creature, shall be able to separate us from the love of God, which is in Christ Jesus our Lord (Romans 8:35,37-39).

Christ alerted His followers to the pressure yet to be brought upon them by other religions (Matthew 10:17), by civil governments (Matthew 10:18), and sadly, by some of their own (2 Thessalonians 4:1ff.). He said: "And ye shall be hated of all men for my name's sake" (Matthew 10:22). History records that Christ's words accurately depicted what was to befall those early saints. As James O. Baird has noted: "In actuality, Christianity was opposed more vigorously than any other religion in the long history of Rome" (1978, p. 29).

Persecution against the church was, and is, rooted in the nature and work of Christ: "But me it hateth, because I testify of it, that its works are evil" (John 7:7). The world hated Christ because of the judgment He brought against what the world is, does, and loves. It will hate those in the church who remind it—by word and by deed— of this judgment. Jesus lamented: "If the world hateth you, ye know that it hath hated me before it hated you" (John 15:18). Hatred often results in persecution. The church, if true to its mission, will be opposed. But Jesus also said:

> Blessed are ye when men shall reproach you, and persecute you, and say all manner of evil against you falsely, for my sake. Rejoice, and be exceeding glad: for great is your reward in heaven: for so persecuted they the prophets that were before you (Matthew 5:11-12).

One thing, however, was beyond doubt. Those saints who remained faithful—even unto death if necessary—would be triumphant (Revelation 2:10). As the great Restorationist, F.G. Allen, so beautifully wrote:

> One by one will we lay our armor down at the feet of the Captain of our salvation. One by one will we be laid away by tender hands and aching hearts to rest on the bosom of Jesus. One by one will our ranks be thus thinned, till erelong we shall all pass over to the other side. But our cause will live. Eternal truth shall never perish. God will look down from His habitation on high, watch over it in His providence, and encircle it in the arms of His love. God will raise up others to take our places; and may we transmit the cause to them in its purity! Though dead, we shall thus speak for generations yet to

come, and God grant that we shall give no uncertain sound! Then may we from our blissful home on high, watch the growth of the cause we love, till it shall cover the whole earth as the waters cover the face of the great deep (1949, pp. 176-177).

Conclusion:
How Humanity Should Serve God

In His manifold dealings with mankind, God consistently has reiterated the fact that, as Sovereign of the Universe, He alone is worthy to be worshipped. When He provided the Israelites with their cherished ten commandments, for example, He reminded them in no uncertain terms:

> I am Jehovah thy God, who brought thee out of the land of Egypt, out of the house of bondage. Thou shalt have no other gods before me. Thou shalt not make unto thee a graven image, nor any likeness of anything that is in heaven above, or that is in the earth beneath, or that is in the water under the earth; thou shalt not bow down thyself unto them; for I Jehovah thy God am a jealous God (Exodus 20:2-5).

It was not enough, however, for man merely to worship God. Through the millennia, God provided specific instructions concerning not only the fact that He was to be worshipped, but the **manner** in which He was to be worshipped. A straightforward reading of the Scriptures reveals that apparently these instructions were set forth very early in human history. The author of the Book of Hebrews substantiated this when he commented on events that transpired shortly after Adam and Eve's expulsion from the Garden of Eden, and the subsequent birth of two of their children, Cain and Abel. The inspired writer observed that "by faith Abel offered unto God a more excellent sacrifice than Cain, through which he had witness borne to him that he was righteous, God bearing witness in respect of his gifts" (Hebrews 11:4).

Whatever else might be gleaned from the Bible's statements about these two brothers, one thing is certain: Abel's worship to God was acceptable; Cain's was not. The conclusion, therefore, is inescapable: Abel had obeyed whatever instructions God had given the first family regarding their worship of Him, while Cain had ignored those same instructions.

These two brothers are not the only siblings from whom such a lesson can be drawn. In the Old Testament Book of Leviticus, the story is told of two of Aaron's sons, Nadab, his firstborn, and Abihu. Leviticus 10 presents a chilling commentary on the two boys' ill-fated attempt to worship God according to their own desires, and not as God had commanded.

> And Nadab and Abihu, the sons of Aaron, took each of them his censer, and put fire therein, and laid incense thereon, and offered strange fire before Jehovah, which he had not commanded them. And there came forth fire from before Jehovah, and devoured them and they died before Jehovah (Leviticus 10:1-2).

The key to understanding the account, of course, is in the fact that they offered "strange fire" that God "had not commanded." Aaron's two sons suffered a horrible death because they ignored Jehovah's specific commands relating to **how** He was to be worshipped.

In referring to the Old Testament, the apostle Paul commented: "For whatsoever things were written aforetime were written for our learning, that through patience and through comfort of the scriptures we might have hope" (Romans 15:4). From the accounts of Cain and Abel, and Nadab and Abihu, we can learn a critically important lesson regarding how God views man's worship of Him. That lesson is this: **God places a premium on foundational knowledge, proper understanding, correct mental attitude, contrite spirit, and reverent obedience** in matters relating to worship offered to Him!

A New Testament example not only bears this out, but brings the matter more clearly into focus. In Matthew 6:1ff., Jesus condemned the Pharisees for their public display of ritualistic religion when He said:

Take heed that ye do not your righteousness before men, to be seen of them: else ye have no reward with your Father who is in heaven. When therefore thou doest alms, sound not a trumpet before thee, as the hypocrites do in the synagogues and in the streets, that they may have glory of men. Verily I say unto you, They have received their reward.... And when ye pray, ye shall not be as the hypocrites: for they love to stand and pray in the synagogues and in the corners of the streets, that they may be seen of men. Verily I say unto you, They have received their reward.... Moreover, when ye fast, be not, as the hypocrites, of a sad countenance: for they disfigure their faces, that they may be seen of men. Verily I say unto you, They have received their reward (Matthew 6:1-2,5,16).

Consider the Pharisees that Christ used as an example of how **not** to worship God. They gave alms; they prayed; they fasted. Under normal circumstances, would each of these acts be acceptable to God? Indeed they would. But the Pharisees performed them for the wrong reason—"to be seen of men." In other words, although the act itself was correct, the **purpose** for which they did it, and the **attitude** with which they did it, were wrong. Hence, **God would not accept their worship!**

Consider also additional New Testament passages that bear on this issue. In 2 Corinthians 9:7, Paul discussed a person's giving of his financial means to the Lord, and stated that "each man" was to "do according as he hath purposed in his heart; not grudgingly, or of necessity: for God loveth a cheerful giver." Both the purpose of the act, as well as the understanding and attitude of the worshiper, were critical. Further, in Luke 22:19, in speaking of the memorial supper that He was instituting, Christ commanded: "This do in remembrance of me." The Scriptures make it clear, however, that it is possible to partake of the Lord's supper in an incorrect way (see 1 Corinthians 11:27-29), thus making it null and void in its effects. In other words, foundational knowledge, proper understanding, correct mental attitude, contrite spirit, and reverent obedience are all vitally important. And when they are missing, the act of worship is vain.

An additional point needs to be examined as well. Sincerity alone is not enough to make an act pleasing and acceptable to God. In 2 Samuel 6, the story is told of a man by the name of Uzzah who was accompanying the Ark of the Covenant of God as it was being moved from one location to another at the command of King David. The Ark had been placed on an ox cart, and the text says simply that "the oxen stumbled" (2 Samuel 6:6). Uzzah—no doubt believing that the precious cargo was about to be tumble from its perch on the cart and be damaged or destroyed—reached up to steady the Ark (2 Samuel 6:6). But Jehovah had commanded that no man, under any circumstances, was to touch the holy things of God (Numbers 4:15). And so, the moment Uzzah touched the Ark, God struck him dead (2 Samuel 6:7).

Was Uzzah sincere in what he did? Undoubtedly. But his sincerity counted for nothing because he disobeyed. Note specifically the Bible's statement that "God smote him there for his **error**" (2 Samuel 6: 7b). God does not want just sincerity; He wants obedience. Jesus Himself said: "If ye love me, ye will keep my commandments" (John 14:15). Furthermore, the way of the Lord is both restrictive and narrow, as Jesus made clear in His beautiful sermon on the mount (read specifically Matthew 7:13-14). In fact, Christ observed: "Not everyone that saith unto me, Lord, Lord, shall enter into the kingdom of heaven; but he that doeth the will of my Father who is in heaven" (Matthew 7:21). Jesus later commented on the attitude of the people of His day when He said: "This people honoreth me with their lips, but their heart is far from me. But in vain do they worship me, teaching as their doctrines the precepts of men" (Matthew 15:8-9).

These people of whom Jesus spoke did not have the foundational knowledge, proper understanding, correct mental attitude, contrite spirit, or reverent obedience God demands of those who would worship and serve Him as He has commanded. There is a valuable lesson in each of these accounts for those of us today who seek to worship and serve God. That lesson is this: we must do **exactly** what God has commanded, in **exactly** the way He has commanded that we do it. Nothing can take the place of simple obedience to the law of God. Neither sincerity nor good intentions will suffice. Only the person who reverently obeys because of adequate foundational knowledge, a proper understanding, a correct mental attitude, and a contrite spirit will be acceptable to God. That being the case, let us all strive not only to worship and serve God, but to worship and serve Him in a scriptural fashion.

REFERENCES

Allen, F.G. (1949), "The Principles and Objects of the Current Reformation," *Foundation Facts and Primary Principles*, ed. G.C. Brewer (Kansas City, MO: Old Paths Book Club).

Baird, James O. (1978), "The Trials and Tribulations of the Church from the Beginning," *The Future of the Church*, ed. William Woodson (Henderson, TN: Freed-Hardeman College).

Bromling, Brad T. (1989), "Jesus—My Lord and My God," *Reasoning from Revelation*, 1[9]:1-2, September.

Bromling, Brad T. (1991a), "Jesus and Jehovah—An Undeniable Link," *Reasoning from Revelation*, 3[2]:3, February.

Bromling, Brad T. (1991b), "The Prophets' Portrait of Christ," *Reason & Revelation*, 11:45-47, December.

Bromling, Brad T. (1995), "Jesus: Truly God and Truly Human," *Reason & Revelation*, 15:17-20, March.

Foster, R.C. (1971), *Studies in the Life of Christ* (Grand Rapids, MI: Baker).

Jackson, Wayne (1979), "Isaiah 53: The Messiah," *Great Chapters of the Bible*, ed. Thomas F. Eaves (Knoxville, TN: East Tennessee School of Preaching and Missions).

Jackson, Wayne (1997a), "Daniel's Prophecy of the 'Seventy Weeks'," *Reason & Revelation*, 17:49-53, July.

Jackson, Wayne (1997b), "The Matter of 'Baptismal Regeneration'," *Christian Courier*, 32:45-46, April.

Jackson, Wayne (1997c), "The Role of 'Works' in the Plan of Salvation," *Christian Courier*, 32:47, April.

Lewis, C.S. (1952), *Mere Christianity* (New York: Macmillan).

Lockyer, Herbert (1973), *All the Messianic Prophecies of the Bible* (Grand Rapids, MI: Zondervan).

McDowell, Josh (1972), *Evidence that Demands a Verdict* (San Bernardino, CA: Campus Crusade for Christ).

McGarvey, J.W. (1875), *The New Testament Commentary: Matthew and Mark* (Delight, AR: Gospel Light).

Robertson, A.T. (1932), *Word Pictures in the New Testament* (Nashville, TN: Broadman).

Schaff, Philip (1910), *History of the Christian Church* (Grand Rapids, MI: Eerdmans).

Schaff, Philip (1913), *The Person of Christ* (New York: American Tract Society).

Schonfield, Hugh J. (1965), *The Passover Plot* (New York: Bantam).

Solomon, David (1972), "Procurator," *Encyclopaedia Judaica*, ed. Cecil Roth (Jerusalem: Keter Publishing).

Stoner, Peter W. and Robert C. Newman (1968), *Science Speaks* (Chicago, IL: Moody).

Thayer, J.H. (1958 reprint), *A Greek-English Lexicon of the New Testament* (Edinburgh: T. & T. Clark).

Thompson, Bert and Wayne Jackson (1992), *A Study Course in Christian Evidences* (Montgomery, AL: Apologetics Press.).

Vine, W.E. (1940), *An Expository Dictionary of New Testament Words* (Old Tappan, NJ: Revell).